DOG WATER FREE
A Memoir

MICHAEL JAY

DOG WATER FREE

First Print Edition

Printed in the United States of America by CreateSpace
Independent Publishing Platform

ISBN: 978-1-9760-5659-8
Library of Congress Control Number: 2017914192
Jay, Michael.
Dog Water Free/Michael Jay
1. Memoir 2. Orphan. 3. Mothers and Sons 4. Non-Fiction

www.dogwaterfree.com

Cover Design by **TOVEY CALL**

To Tommy
And to his daughter and to his son, Amy and Tom, Jr.
And to everyone who loved him.

DISCLAIMER

DOG WATER FREE is a memoir about a journey to find emotional truth. These are the author's recollections. To protect the privacy of others, some names have been changed. In two minor incidences (regarding Mikee's 2 St. Bernard's), events have been condensed. Otherwise, these events are as the author remembers them to have happened. Any resemblance to fictional events or to fictitious persons is entirely coincidental.

CONTENTS

"Automobile in America,
Chromium steel in America,
Wire-spoke wheel in America,
Very big deal in America!"

-Lyrics by Stephen Sondheim

ONE

DUMBFOUNDED

Legends are born to every generation. In cities and towns, the world over, stories of glory are passed from fathers and mothers to sons and daughters.

I am collecting mine now.

At Augusta, Jack Nicklaus will defend his first Masters when the azaleas bloom in April.

Out in Los Angeles, Sandy Koufax and Don Drysdale are still basking in the glory of the Dodger's sweep of the Yankees last fall. They held the two-time defending champs to four runs in four games.

Down in Miami, an up-and-comer by the name of Cassius Clay will be a 7-1 underdog to Sonny Liston at the end of the month, according to my little brother, who somehow knows about such things. The challenger pays no mind. Preening before a bouquet of microphones, he can't resist taunting one of the meanest fighters in the history of the sport. "He's too *ugly* to be champion of the world. The champ should be *pretty*...like me." He is also composing a poem for the occasion. I can't wait for the weigh-in.

Up in Toronto, the Leafs are on the brink of a third consecutive Cup, but they'll have to get by my Wings to do it, so I pray to God they don't.

Back stateside in Midtown over at New York City Center, rehearsals are underway for a second revival of *West Side Story* when John, Paul, George and Ringo step down onto the tarmac at JFK. Frenzy is fueling hysteria as an onslaught of flashbulbs warms an otherwise lackluster February sky. In living rooms across America, the music of Leonard Bernstein is about to earn a breather. Turntables will rest when families gather to watch a band called The Beatles on *Ed Sullivan*, about which I am clueless. Except for knowing that the girls in our neighborhood are all abuzz, I just learned that our dad is going to join us on the couch on Sunday for some TV viewing that doesn't involve a prizefight or a bowling tournament or *The Untouchables*. So it must be big.

South of Manhattan at Arlington National, on the outskirts of our nation's Capital, the eternal flame is marking a snow-covered grave. It's been almost three months since sixth-graders like me felt eerily responsible for our numbing sadness as we watched a little boy hero salute his father's flag-draped coffin. Hard as I try, it is impossible to imagine how he must have been feeling. God love him.

Meanwhile, in a working-class neighborhood in the heart of Detroit's Westside, a young mom is receiving news from her doctor. She has a year to prepare her family for her death. She will be leaving the man she loves and the four children she cherishes behind to fend for themselves.

Nearby, neighbors don't know what to say.

Heartfelt prayers fill voids of silence. *"God help them,"* they are heard to mutter.

Still on her mission fifteen months later, her focus heightens when her husband drops dead.

Some wonder aloud what many are thinking. "What in the world could this family have done to deserve a fate such as this?"

Everyone wants to know.

Outside, the rain pounds.

Inside, candles flicker while mourners pack into pews. Late arrivals hug the walls as a mist of incense shrouds friends and faithful. Schoolchildren join in quiet prayer. "Kyrie, eleison. Christe, eleison."

Lord, have mercy…Christ, have mercy.

Dumbfounded, I'm standing in the vestibule.

My name is Mikee and I am one befuddled, sorry mess of an eighth-grader.

I'm pretty sure that I'm suffering from something called *impostor-syndrome* for having spent way too much time in church reciting Latin, but not actually praying.

It sounded so harmless that I should be appointed "President of the Altar Boys."

Thank you, Sisters. They did it to honor my mom. And I must admit that it pleased her to no end when they put *me* in charge of a contingent of Mass-servers in our parish.

I am just now realizing I was blindsided.

My duties are endless. Much of it involves handing down edicts from the nuns. Latin must be enunciated. Mumbles don't cut it. Servers have to show up fifteen minutes in advance. Shoes must be wiped of mud before entering the sacristy. And they had better be dress shoes. No sneakers. Priests will verify. And altar boys must at least *look* prayerful, so bed-head is verboten. *Check. Check. Check.* They've also put me in charge of scheduling, which is a mixed blessing since it allows me to slot myself for weddings to earn a little cash on Saturdays, as if weekday and Sunday Mass-serving duties aren't enough.

I've also begun serving as many funerals as possible for the chance to enjoy some fine second-hand cigar smoke while riding in the back of cushy Cadillacs with the Monsignor and missing huge chunks of school. Burials at cemeteries like Mt. Olivet over on the Eastside can keep me absent from the nuns until well past noon on those days. So that's how bad it's become. I now look forward to funerals, for God's sake, which I have come to view as *mini-vacations.* Lord help me.

Most mornings, I'm in the sacristy at this hour, waiting for an elbow from the priest to let me know that it's time to look respectful, as I march toward the altar. There will be no such nudge on this day, however. Today, there will be only the sound of a dirge.

An organ blast from the balcony above will signal our time to roll.

Paced by pallbearers, we shuffle arm-in-arm up the center aisle, my two brothers, my sister, my mom and me.

The sight of our dad's casket before us is giving rise to speculation.

Murmurs are blanketing the congregation.

A secret is passing among them.

God help us.

TWO

PEACE AND OUT

I blamed it on one too many furtive glances when time stood still again eight months later.

The clock on the wall of our eighth-grade homeroom froze like a rope on a forgotten toboggan after a cold night face down on a hill. Then, with one last desperate tock, life imitated a cartoon when its hands spun like a pinwheel before falling limp on the six. Fretful classmates notwithstanding, the drone from whirring sprockets had me grinning. I figured it somewhat sublime on this final day of our elementary school careers that our black-rimmed *Seth Thomas* should join the ranks of those with nothing left to give. *Hasta la vista, good Sisters of the Order of St. Dominic.*

Peace and out, Seth.

Placing my faith in the bell, I retreat to another world. Need be, I'll just say *"I'm heading out for a loaf of bread,"* if anyone asks, before I hop on the bus over to Michigan and Trumbull when Mantle and Maris and the Yankees come to town. I'll get up early on that July fifth morning to beat the crowds to watch our homegrown Tommy Tresh play a little pepper with his teammate Mick. Then I'll watch them both shag flies and sling their own brands of frozen ropes to the bag at second from deep in the Tiger outfield. Any big leaguer can chase down a high fly, of course. It's the throw that follows that makes my tail wag. It's all about anticipation, and keeping your head in the game and thoughtful footwork to position for momentum *before* the ball is in your glove. So I'm learning. Ah, summer. Balloons will bob from our backyard clothesline on my upcoming fourteenth birthday. There will be no cake and no ice cream on that mid-July afternoon, I've just decided. With help from my mom, we'll serve up a screwball. My little *par-tay* will mark a departure. It'll forever be remembered for *Red n' Yellow* side-by-side, just cherry pie and corn on the cob sharing the same paper plate. That should get a rise out of the girls in the neighborhood. God, I can hardly wait. Summer at last. On evenings when I don't have a game, I'll walk the ball fields across from our house with my little Duchess, stride for stride. We'll check out every backstop to scout the competition and visit with faithful fans. At the age of six months, my Old English sheepdog has become a total babe magnet, by the way. Who knew? When I'm not rolling around on the lawn with my best buddy or firing up our mower, I'll be across the street shagging flies myself — or at the plate taking my swats. Maybe this year I'll learn how to lay off high inside fastballs. I dream. Cue the ringer. Clock dismissed. Summer vacation at last.

Two weeks pass in a blink.

Birds were flying low beneath a darkening midday sky when I learned the sorry truth about what it means for a boy to man a shovel. And I thought math was hard.

Even my blisters wept that day.

Had it not been for my mom standing nearby, I would never have managed. Resting her wrists on my shoulders, she looked me in the eye. *"Come on, Mikee. You dig. I'll pray. I'm not going anywhere."*

She made me do it with those exact words. And in time, her insistence would prove to be a godsend; for had she been any less resolute that day, I would have no doubt remained forever unmindful of a much bigger truth that no one in the world could know. My puppy isn't all I buried on that tear-filled eighth-grade afternoon in June when I said good-bye to my beautiful Duchess.

"Not bad for a first-timer with a shovel," my mom offered, with a smile just right and a hug for good measure. *"Hold onto your dear mother here, mister."* Two simple graveside prayers later, she leaned into my shoulder to give my arm a loving squeeze. *"It's ok to be sad, buddy,"* she whispered, just as my tears came flooding.

Intended or not, with that lesson in closure behind me, I could feel my confidence grow. And by the time my blisters callused, I had become all but certain I could handle just about anything life threw at me.

Until tonight.

THREE

FAYED

Desperate, I cling to a memory from back in the day, hoping against hope it might bring me solace, since it never failed to work its magic in the face of bleak circumstance in the past. I'm remembering my little brother as a precocious first-grader. Whenever storm clouds gathered or our mom got riled, Patrick knew just how to break the tension with a whisper of his own. He resorts to pig Latin to avoid breaking an oath and incurring our mom's wrath. *"I guess this means we're uck-fayed, don't it, Mikee?"* I laugh. Thank God. I'm all better. Sort of.

So why am I thrashing so?

And how did these past months flash by in such a flurry? And what's up with this evil chill that's now slicing my fifteen-year-old body in half? I'm shaking like some lame little imp is dancing a jig atop a grave that's somewhere in my own future. We're talking dire and frantic foreboding here, as I stand on this funeral home landing. *Lord, help me.* My dad is dead. My puppy has been put down and buried. And tonight my mom lies lifeless on a heavy steel gurney in a dark lonesome recess of the basement below. With all that I'm feeling, I wouldn't be a bit surprised if I woke up dead tomorrow too. Might as well join the party. Whatever. I'm ready. I think.

I can't stop obsessing.

You do wake up after you die, don't ya?

Jesus, Mikee.

Settle, already.

Comfort finds me by way of another distant memory. I can feel the mellow timbre of his inflection in my bones. Such a soothing Belfast-born lilt it is when my grandfather spins tales that are true. Most often, he speaks of the lineage of bred offspring of famous racehorses and where they fit in the history of the *Sport of Kings*. He talks about thoroughbreds with names like Gallant Fox and Citation, or Seabiscuit, sired by Hard Tack, son of Man o' War, the most famous chestnut of all. And when he is spot-on his game, we hear about *his* own offspring, like his courageous and gutsy Margaret Mary, a chestnut in her own right, otherwise known as my mom Marge.

And so it is. In the spirit of the words of my mom's father who knows a thing or two about lineage, *'tis enough to make me remember how it all began*…eight short years before…when bewilderment was my friend.

FOUR

FATE

An unflappable muse, motherhood becomes her. As mood maven and mentor to her budding brood of four, everyone who knows Marge loves her for her sparkle. A spirited gamer with a secret, she styles through matters mundane with the passion of a virtuoso readying for Carnegie Hall. But for the size of her heart, the Irish in her bones, and the grace of God, she might never have evolved with such consummate charm. Too bad for me. It complements her all-too-disconcerting intuition, which allows her to predict what her favorite second-grader is going to do before I can even think about doing it. More perplexing still is something I learned during a recent moment of confidence. My very own most faithful, happily married mom has a mysterious schoolgirl crush on Mr. Spooky himself.

I don't get it.

Our Magnavox *pings* before casting its warm glow. That's when the creepiest man on television hits his mark. Deadpan cool, Rod Serling becomes one with the camera. Prone to the willies, I shudder to think he might be standing in our living room when he speaks about a dimension...not only of sight and sound...but of mind...beyond that which is known to man...as vast as space and as timeless as infinity...in a middle ground...between light and shadow...science and superstition...somewhere between the pit of man's fears and the summit of his knowledge...beyond the boundaries of imagination...in a place called...*wait for it...*

Nannah-Nannah — Nannah-Nannah...

THE TWILIGHT ZONE!

Please give it up already, mister! God, that music creeps me out. As for Marge, she can't get enough of his confident swagger when he weaves issues of human nature into his freakazoid fables, none of which I am old enough to fathom nor quite young enough to ignore. "Come on, Mikee. Sit with me here. Let's watch this." She pats the couch. A master of all manner of maternal prerogative, she loves nothing more than testing my mettle.

"Aw, come on Mom. Must we?" I mean it.

Bone-chilled after a sweaty walk home following Friday night hockey on the pond, I oblige by burrowing my head into a sofa cushion. A throw finds my shoulders.

"Look at you. You're shivering. Here you go, buddy." She swaddles me.

I thank her though it doesn't help.

Except for Jack Paar, which I'm never awake to see, Mister Creepy Spooky there and *Alfred Hitchcock Presents* are the only TV shows Marge enjoys. I don't know which is worse. Best I can tell; they both fuel her delight in crafting beguiling challenges, which tickles her fancy big-time. It makes for a baptism of absolute befuddlement for me, her devoted but clueless third-born middle son. *Nannah-Nannah — Nannah-Nannah.* That wacked-out music won't stop playing in my head.

Welcome to the *MikeeZone*.

In a neighborhood of a town brimming as much with peril as promise, all I know is how to ride a two-wheeler and when to genuflect during Mass. Oh yeah, I've also reached the *Age of Reason*. At last. I'm off the bench. At the venerable age of seven, they've put me in the game. Absent is that cloud with no hint of silver lining that had been hovering over my head. Now endowed with *Free Will*, gone is certain destiny that would have me spend eternity in a *NeverLand* called Purgatory, which the nuns promise is not as horrible as the torment of hell, but dreadful nonetheless, *"since it's not quite Heaven, children."* No wonder we all counted the days until First Holy Communion.

Heading home with a spotless soul after making my First Confession, I can't resist closing my eyes and swinging for the fences.

"LORDTAKEMENOW," I blurt untainted, as I duck into a shrub for mortal cover.

Dumbstruck, I still don't know whether to feel lucky or sad that the hand of God stayed put that day.

So I guess I got that going for me.

Meanwhile, Marge indulges her ever-loving instinct by entangling me in a perfectly exigent web. Believing a well-timed challenge can make a good boy a better man, she concocts a summertime doozy of a notion in honor of my upcoming eighth year.

She calls it *disappearing.*

I call it unbelievable.

Within reason, she tells me, I will never again have to ask her permission to go anywhere or do anything.

Huh?

As long as I promise to obey the law, to steer clear of a nearby public housing project, and to return home by an appointed late afternoon hour, I can *disappear* whenever I darn well please. Imagine. With that, rather than feeling like somebody wants me out of her hair, my buttons are popping for having earned her trust, which I swear never to squander.

Planting my face deep in the screen as I blast through the door, I'm out before she can change her mind. *Free at last.* Inside the garage, I imagine hearing my grandfather's hurried brogue as I push off atop my Schwinn with no fenders. *Moykee. Look at ya. Ya little shite. Ya got yourself a fookin' hall pass, don't ya?* I laugh. I am well into my crooked roll down the driveway when Marge steps onto our front porch to launch her parting salvo. It hovers in the air...like a slow belch from a cold-morning smokestack downriver. "Hey. Have fun out there, buddy, but do me a favor. Promise me you will never tempt fate, especially on a dare. I'm serious."

Huh?

There's not a soul in our neighborhood old enough to ride a bike who doesn't know about dares. That much I get. It's the other part of her caution that puts me in a tailspin as I pedal toward the high school on our corner. I'm about to step into *the cove* for an afternoon of three-wall rubber-ball fast-pitch when it hits me. *Who the heck is this guy Fate anyhow and what is his flipping problem anyway?*

I'm serious.

Time tempers my innocence. Within a handful of years, one thing has become clear. In our little corner of America, slim is the difference between survival and disaster. That's why you do not crawl under a car sitting up on a spindle of a jack to retrieve a thirty-nine cent rubber ball. You do not accept a dare to jump a freight train moving a hair faster than you can run. You do not swim during *polio season*. You do not crouch behind the plate if you are not wearing a cup. And needless to say, you do not ride on a wooden roller coaster called *"The Wild Beast"* after a disturbing mishap had it condemned by city officials, even when invited to do so by your fifth-grade sweetheart's father at the annual *DPOA Family Day Outing*, hosted by the Detroit Police Officers' Association over at Edgewater Park.

Perhaps most obvious to an altar boy like me in the 1960s, you never accept a dare to touch a communion wafer with your hands unless you *want* God to throw a lightning bolt down upon you.

"God made 'em flunk me," shouted one fallen acolyte. Although not quite a bolt of lightning, that boy heard a serious thunderclap when the nuns held him back a grade for munching on hosts while scarfing sips of *Manischewitz* from the cupboard in the sacristy.

That was around the time something happened that affected everyone who knew us. It led to that late morning shuffle up the center aisle behind my dad's casket. It was a week into my eighth-grade year when I learned the real truth about the perils of tempting fate.

In get-it-done style, I heard my dad give an order. He was talking to someone he called *an associate*, on whom I had never before laid eyes. With unmistakable clarity, he instructed that cologne-laden wise guy to direct a stonecutter to prepare a grave marker before its time.

"Gimme a break. Are you saying he won't do it because he needs more information? I gave him all I got for now. You just tell that little mook that I need him to get started," I heard my dad tell him.

Done and done.

Sure enough, in a matter of weeks, that was that.

Now, the convergence of recent events would make you think I had accepted a dare to crowbar the poorbox from the vestibule of our church. God help me. It hasn't even been a full day since we said our good-byes, my mom and me.

I miss her already.

Ignoring the consequences, I flip off fate when I tell myself my situation cannot get worse.

Aw, Mikee…Mikee….

Big mistake.

I knew it as soon as I said it.

Would I ever fookin' learn?

How could I have forgotten the anguish on the face of that diminutive stonemason whose reluctant desire to do a favor for a small-fry goombah sent events into a spiral two years before? Flush against the funeral parlor wall, he sat with a cadre of men that I never before had seen. All dressed to the nines, they joined in quiet prayer. Short-brimmed hats in hand, they looked like brothers of Green Bay's coach Lombardi in their long tweed topcoats. Beads dangled from their chins as they pressed small crucifixes against their lips. Murmuring in unison, their plea sounded like something I learned as a Mass server, but different.

"O come molto triste...

Come molto sbadato...

Come molto stupido...

Antonio...Antonio...Antonio."

Other than clergy, no one in that dim lit room appeared more comfortable with their surroundings than that well-tailored group of men on the night of my dad's Rosary. Quick to pay homage before the service began, their prayerful, not-quite-Latin chant made it feel like Satan himself might be channeling their words in English, lurking among them, plotting and laughing.

"*Oh how very sad....*

Oh how very careless....

Oh how very stupid...Tony...Tony...Tony."

Five Hail Marys in, the strangers in overcoats vanished without notice.

All I could do was pray to God that they took the Devil with them.

Now my brother's eyes are burning holes in the windshield. Hands on ten and two, his white-knuckle grip on the wheel of our two-year-old '66 Fury belies our 12-mph pace. We're in a crawl fest down side streets to our neighborhood funeral home on this last day of March. *Come on, Nino. Drive, will ya?* Absent conversation, I do what I do. I fiddle. An anthem breaks the stony silence. Thank God for pinholes in the dash. *"Heaven holds a place for those who pray...hey-hey-hey."* Rolling past our Catholic Church, the lyrics turn prophetic. *"...Look around you, all you see are sympathetic eyes...."*

Good timing, that. I'll never feel at home with sympathy. Nino is learning to thrive on it. Three years my senior, we're polar opposites that way for good reason, my older bro and me. We've grown up apart. At eighteen, he has already spent five years behind seminary walls, studying for the priesthood. And praying for peace.

God knows he deserves it.

As for me at this moment, it seems that I merit something else altogether.

I'm upside down. Awash in dread, I can't stop picturing the scene at the bottom of the stairs. I'm drowning here. That I should know just what to expect in the basement below makes my heart skip. It's pumping like it wants out. Was it just two years ago as an awkward eighth-grader that I struggled to stand strong to support my mom when she picked out a casket for my dad? And how is it that tonight I am standing by myself, about to do the same for her?

"Eat me fate," I curse through a window at the evening sky above. Being alone on this night was never supposed to be part of the plan.

Lord. God. Help me.

Thirty hours ago, I wasn't alone. The hallway at the hospital had grown crowded with people. All gathered to be near Marge at the end. She made new friends every day, so it should have come as no surprise when nurses, housekeeping assistants and a contingent of medical students assembled. Administrators and a blush of young candy stripers joined in quiet tribute.

As proud as that made me, it took a toll on Nino, who has refused to utter a word since yesterday when we left the hospital. Despite having so much to discuss, he would have none of it. Arriving at our destination, I know one thing for sure. If ever I needed my big brother to step up and stay strong, it's now.

The sight of the entry stops us in our tracks. Cars are whooshing by. Nino is standing as if in a trance, arms dangling by his sides.

"I'll get the door," I offer.

Mmmmmf.

The harder I pull the slower it moves.

A boy less clueless would have seen that as an omen. I should have known I was about to begin the longest night of my young life.

The aroma of gladiolas confirms we're entering a neighborhood institution. I hold my breath to keep from gagging. An attendant point to an office.

Looking like an undertaker, the owner sits ramrod straight. His manicured hands are lying flat in a pool of task light atop a desk so massive it makes everything else in the room appear small. Ready for business, he gestures toward a pair of wingbacks. Set at forty-fives, they're a bit too close to the desk front for comfort. Damning the smells, I suck some air. No turning back, in we shuffle. As the owner cranes to look past us for the adult in the transaction, I glance at Nino. He looks like I feel. Despondent and broken. Eyes shut, he shakes his head.

I begin by thanking the man for a glass of water. Nino grabs the box of Kleenex. I tell the owner our name. I tell him that we live in the neighborhood. I tell him that our mom passed away the day before. I have no clue that he had earlier taken a call from the morgue.

"Your mother is already downstairs, boys," he advises.

It's way too much information.

Nino's shudder makes me tremble. I rub his back. I tell him that we'll be ok. "We've got to stick together," I whisper. I've never felt closer to him than at this moment, sitting knee-to-knee. Thank God, we have each other.

Now that he has our full attention, the owner settles in. His detached tone makes it sound like he's reading a trusty bedtime story.

He talks about process and selection of a casket.

Okay.

He suggests the type of clothing Marge should wear.

Okay.

He inquires about pallbearers as he shifts his gaze to Nino, who has still yet to utter a word. "Ah, now, before we continue, why don't *you* tell me, young man, which *adult* will be coming by to finalize these matters?" The owner's stare cuts right through him.

Please don't go there, mister.

Ashen, Nino looks like a wisp of spent dandelion blowing around the outfield. *Come on. Stick with me here. Stick with me here, Nino.*

It ain't workin'.

Sobbing, he bolts from the building. "I can't do it. I just can't do it."

His bawling makes my head drop into my hands. Elbows on my knees, I'm grateful to be hidden by the vast expanse of mahogany desktop. I stare at my sneakers. I have to remind myself to breathe. For the first time in my life, I'm the kid at the far end of the bench hoping the coach *won't* call my name.

Staying low, I pray for time. Nonplussed, the owner obliges. Without a word, he opens a drawer to ignore me as he tends to paperwork.

Nino will be back. I'm sure of it. He just needs some air. Brothers do not desert brothers. Not like this. No way. Not like this.

A heartbeat later, a spray of gravel clicks and tumbles. Tires squeal.

Nino is history.

That hurts.

Rising from behind his desk, the owner stands before me, a funeral home director in all his glory. It's back to business. I'm still seated, doubled over, desperate to focus on my shoes.

"Okay, let's try this again, shall we?" he engages. "Please, young man, I need some help here. Who will be handling these details, and who will be picking out this casket?"

Breathe, Mikee.

I look up. "That would be me, sir." I say it as if Marge can still hear my words.

She *can* still hear my words, can't she? I wonder if anyone knows for sure. Screw it. All that matters now is that *I* know what *I* need to believe to put this task behind me. *Of course, she can hear me.*

At the end of a hall, a wide metal door leads to the landing where the stairway to the basement looms.

Promises came easy when I told Marge that I could handle this. I assured her that I would enlist Nino's help. No biggie. Not to worry, we would be there for each other, me and Nino. Of course, we'd keep our sister out of it. That was then. Now, even my feet are sad and confused. Desperate for traction, I tell myself that I've never met a basement I didn't like, since every house in our neighborhood has a basement. Basements are where kids play floor hockey in socks, while furnaces rumble and laundry dries. Basements are where moms do *mom-things*, like ironing, while kids work on science fair projects. Basements are where dance parties happen and where first kisses become lifelong memories.

Ah, good one, Mikee. That's better.

Then I reach the bottom step.

An acrid stench reminds me this basement holds happy memories for no one. The stink of embalming fluids makes heavy curtains reek. Beyond the veils, an elevator services a corridor of workstations where the living meets the dead. Helpers with trays of cosmetics attend to the departed to make them look like they are just taking naps. Except for reasons of facial disfigurement, open casket viewings are the absolute rule in our Westside neighborhood.

Torchiere floor lamps and tracks of canister lights create a showroom atmosphere. Chemical vapors make my eyes water. Chrome handles glow and silky interiors glisten. I strain to focus. No price tags, not even one. Then I remember. They don't tell you the price until you pick one. A whisper tickles the back of my neck. "…This one here has a 50-year waterproof guarantee, son."
Do I look that helpless?

Steeled by his up-sell, I choose. Marge gets a plain, low-luster beige model with long hollow handles. It's the most nondescript casket on the floor. As for lining, pale rose faux satin works for me. I feel better about my choice when the owner refers to the casket's interior as "Glossy Pink Sateen." He makes it sound luxurious. I can almost hear Marge laugh. She could have cared less about frills. All she wanted was that I make her proud by enlisting the help of my older brother and doing what we could to save on cost. I am sure she would have approved.

At least the owner has done his homework. "On the morning of the funeral, we'll meet here and ride to the church together. After the Mass at St. Suzanne's, the interment will be at Holy Sepulcher, out on Ten Mile and Telegraph. Your mother, Margaret Mary, will be buried in a plot right next to your father, Anthony John," he promises. Back upstairs, he extends his arm to touch my shoulder when he shakes my hand.

"You've done a good job here, son," he tells me.

I want to puke.

Out on the street I draw a breath so deep I surprise myself. I feel like I've been underwater. I am back at Marge's deathbed. She is calm, just as she was when she told my dad and my sister and brothers and me about her diagnosis four years before, back when I was eleven. *We can't be certain, but it looks like six months to a year, perhaps a bit more,* the doctors all told her. It was then that she resurrected calling me by a nickname that she had settled on when I was a tot.

I am pulling her out the door. I'm telling her about a dead thing that I'd found, the first I had ever seen. A bald, gray birdie with a tiny yellow beak lay splattered on the broom-swept concrete below a nest inside our garage. Chirps and peeps echoed in the rafters on the day I became her sparrow. Talking nonstop, Marge scrapes up the little mess. She tells me that I'm smart and observant. She tells me that she's proud of me. Otherwise engaged, I hear not a word. I'm mesmerized by an army of ants marching in straight-line formation toward that ooze of sparrow splatter. Such a spectacle. It's nothing short of fantastic for a boy almost five....

Those were the days.

Breathe, Mikee. Breathe.

It's a trudge of a slow trod home. I imagine Marge at our kitchen table. She is sipping her coffee, insisting that we talk about my future. It's the week after I learned of her illness. She's telling me about something that she calls *"a promise of the universe."* She is making it sound like the roller coaster of events in my life are part of a destiny. She is saying everything is happening for a reason and that it will all fall into place.

At that moment, it made me feel better.

Now, I am not certain of anything.

All I know for sure tonight is that I am alone.

I cannot stop my mind from churning. What if this nightmare isn't real?

What if...*Stay still, Mikee. Pull up the covers. Roll onto your side. Close your eyes. Deep breath. There will be time to make sense of it all...starting at the very beginning...in the morning. Go back to sleep.*

That's better.

It must be a dream.

FIVE

AMUSED AT FIRST SIGHT

DETROIT 1945

Picture Emeril Lagasse in his starched kitchen whites and you would have the image of my dad in his work attire. Given their facial resemblance and modest stature, Chef Tony and Chef Emeril could have been brothers by blood.

Marge, on the other hand, is a statuesque auburn-haired beauty. A proud member of the tribe of Maureen O'Hara, she and her favorite actress were mistaken for sisters often. As for her forthright demeanor, a young Katherine Houghton Hepburn hits the mark.

Empowered by a strict upbringing, Marge evolves as a self-styled patrician. Most engaging is her endearing self-confidence, which allows her to laugh at herself often. As she's taller than Tony by more than two inches, he compensates for his height with a playful personality. Marge finds him engaging, in a curious sort of way, though no Archibald Leach is he.

First-generation Americans both, my dad and mom were born into families that hailed from Warsaw, I think, and the far reaches of Ireland. Like most offspring of immigrants who had traded the dark days of Europe for America's Great Depression, in their homes they were taught to endure. Food on the table and a roof over their heads is all that matters in these neighborhoods, where professions of parents can put a lid on one's dreams forever. In most cases, if breadwinners are laborers, children follow suit. With few exceptions, survival is the paramount goal if your father is a working-class sort. Marge's dad is on the production line downriver at Mr. Henry Ford's pride and joy, the largest heavy manufacturing complex in the world. An industrial behemoth, *The Rouge* is home to 75,000 workers, 27 miles of conveyors and 53,000 separate pieces of machinery. It's a factory like no other. Also at home with noise, heat, fumes and dust in the workplace, Tony's dad forges steel at a foundry.

Detroit's neighborhoods would soon be populated with public high schools that have names like Denby, Mumford, Cody, Northwestern and Mackenzie. There is also Cooley High, which Marge attends.

Supplementing core curriculums, most offer vocational studies in woodworking, automotives, and culinary arts. To Tony's credit, he breaks the father-son factory-work cycle by studying commercial food preparation at Detroit Chadsey.

For reasons unknown, he never graduates from high school, nor does he become a war hero. Deferred from military service, he finds quick work at a downtown grille, where he proves capable as a *short order*. Soon thereafter, he catches a break when he is brought on as a line-cook at a somewhat fashionable restaurant in a residential hotel that has a reputation for careful hiring.

Standing tall in the heart of Detroit's Cultural and Medical Center area, the twelve-story Belcrest Hotel opened its doors in 1926, and now, nearly two decades later, its attentive staff is still serving an upscale clientele, which suits Tony to a tee. His self-deprecating charm and work ethic play to his advantage. As a first generation, Polish American who thrives on acceptance, he mixes with ease within the broad range of cultures that work there by making everyone, even management, feel like they have found a new best friend. And since he punches a clock, he doesn't mind working long hours.

Marge begins waitressing a couple of years later.

With a shape and style that makes her off-the-rack uniform look tailored, she captivates diners with her poise and grace. It's reflected in the size of her tips, which become legendary among the staff. Toss in a joyful hip swivel and a smile that lights up the room and no guy in the place can resist her.

"Hi, I'm Tony. So how's work treating ya?" He smiles as if he knows something she doesn't.

No stranger to unwanted advances, Marge replies with a single deep sigh as she clears a cluttered four top. Before he can ask her name, she is off.

At his locker the next morning, he buffs a pair of fresh-out-of-the-box shoes. He had purchased them weeks before on a promise that they would give him two extra inches. Avoiding the rubber mats in front of his cook top, he gives his thick soles a graze on the wide-grout terra cotta. God forbid a slip should cause a mishap. Soles scuffed, he's ready to work some Tony magic.

Like most mornings, Marge makes her way through the empty dining room at the stroke of ten-fifty-five. Tony appears from nowhere as she sashays through a maze of tables. Moving closer, chin held high, he is concentrating on walking tall when it happens. Powerless to take his eyes off her, he stumbles into a full-blown header.

"Damn lifts," he mutters.

Flat on his belly, he's lucky he didn't crack his skull on the edge of a serving station. Peeking out from beneath a table, Tony pretends to be retrieving something from the floor. "Ah, uh, so how ya doin'?"

Marge smiles in reply. *For the love of Pete, you cannot be serious. Who is this strange little man and how can I not treat this creature with mercy?*

Oddly charmed, she cannot resist engaging. "Are you talking to me?" she asks, while staring at the man who looks like he's wearing a floppy linen bonnet as he sneaks a peek out from the darkness down under.

"Hi, Tony. I'm Marge and I'm doing well. Thanks for asking. Say, I bet you'd like to take me to dinner at the best place in town. Isn't that what you've been wanting to do?" she teases. "I have tomorrow night off, by the way."

Heading home that evening, Tony cannot resist congratulating himself. "You have quite a way with the ladies, mister."

It sums up Tony to a tee.

In his own mind, he is a legend.

The next day, he calls every contact in his universe to get a dinner reservation at Detroit's famed London Chop House.

As they approach the reception stand, his hand is on the small of Marge's back. The maitre d' offers a courteous bow. When Tony says, "Good evening," he realizes that he had never before spoken to someone wearing a tuxedo. They are shown to a curved leather banquette. A booth-placard greets them. *"Reserved for Tony the Chef."*

So far so good.

A warm plate of breads joins a chilled silver bowl of creamed herring at the center of the table. A crystal bud vase holds a single red rose. The waiter uncorks two splits of champagne. He calls it a gesture of welcome, compliments of the house. The glow of candlelight makes it all feel like a dream. Never has Tony felt so relaxed in a restaurant after having been recognized as *a chef* for the first time in his life. He is resplendent in a padded-shouldered, charcoal-gray, double-breasted suit, solid dark tie and matching pocket square. A starched white shirt, silver cufflinks and a brilliant black shine on his shoes complete his ensemble. Sitting next to the most beautiful girl in the place makes him feel like a genuine celebrity, despite a momentary worry that he may have slapped on too much aftershave. Hours later at the bar, conversation flows.

They dance until morning.

Working together in the hotel restaurant and lounge, late nights are common and alcohol is plentiful. It doesn't take long for Marge to start helping Tony and the bartender close the place. On those nights, they drink until they can't stand up.

With Marge in the lineup, Tony gains stature when a handful of athletes, media-wary politicians, and small-time racketeers decide that *closing the place* should become their ritual as well. And despite their obvious enchantment with the cook's girlfriend, Marge keeps her focus by schooling Tony on how to create precious social currency as an after-hours gatekeeper. He relishes every minute. He loves the attention he gains from the big shots almost as much as he loves having Marge by his side. For the first time in his life, the stars are aligning. The Red Wings are in the Stanley Cup Finals. By August, World War II ends and the Tigers are playing their way into the '45 World Series. Business is booming and spirits are high. It makes for a glamorous courtship for a couple of kids like Tony and Marge, living the dream, in the heart of a city that has everything going for it.

It's not long before Marge begins to see Tony as the future father of her children. The extent of her commitment reveals itself when she volunteers to convert to Catholicism for her husband-to-be. While it hasn't even occurred to Tony to ask her to do so, she knows his family expects it, just as she knows it will cause heartburn on her side of the aisle. As the stubborn daughter of a staunch *Orangeman*, Marge chooses to deal with the issue of her conversion by telling her Protestant father, *"This is just the way it's gotta be."*

Tony cannot believe his good fortune. The woman stealing his heart is not only beautiful but wise beyond her years. Bursting with ideas, Marge gives him direction with ease, which is also something he cherishes. In that regard, he isn't a complicated guy. Tony doesn't mind working. He just doesn't like to think. So Marge does the thinking for both of them. On the heels of a whirlwind romance, fueled by their mutual affinity for socializing and drinking, they're married. It begins a time when Marge has but one thing on her mind. It's a desire she only whispers. And whenever she does, it makes Tony delirious.

"I want babies."

In 1946, they welcome a daughter. It marks the start of Marge's occupation as *baby-namer-in-chief* as Tony becomes the sole breadwinner of a soon-to-be growing family.

SIX

FOUR KIDS, FOUR FAMILIES

Boomers all, Kathleen Sheila, Anthony John and Michael Jay are born three years apart. The baby of the family, Patrick Jerome, comes along twenty months after me.

Tony defers to Marge on all things having to do with their daughter, Kathleen, which sets the tone for what is to come. She is their princess. She has her own bedroom and a shelf full of books. She has her own record collection.

.She has a portable hi-fi, which looks like a piece of hard luggage when the lid is clasped. She also enjoys spending time with a great group of girlfriends, most of whom are teammates from the grade school swim team. Since they practice indoors at the public high at the end of our street, her friends are at our house often. Marge loves hosting Friday night sleepover-dance parties that keep our basement off-limits to my brothers and me. Regardless, there is still plenty to hear from behind our hollow kitchen door at the top of the stairs. The sound of our mom joining along with Connie Francis to sing, *"Where the Boys Are,"* is enough to make us sneak out the side door to lie on our bellies on the driveway and spy through the basement window. The girls that aren't "doing each other's hair," or munching chips and sipping Cokes through straws are in a swoon-fest, laughing and dancing, while Marge empties bags of ice into our laundry tub.

The oldest boy, nicknamed *Nino,* is baptized *Anthony John,* after our dad. In the unfortunate tradition of unlucky namesakes, he is doomed to fail in meeting his father's expectations. For all Tony cares, their relationship requires too much effort. Over-matched, Tony is incapable of accepting a soft-spoken son who has brains and good looks, but no interest in sports or roughneck behavior. An all-A student, Nino is a well-pressed sort of boy with needs that far exceed his dad's sensibilities. As a father of the Fifties, homophobic rants are not at all uncommon. Imbued with a manner fitting a tough but none-too-smart delinquent bound for Juvenile Hall, Tony makes his position clear when he announces that boys should be all about roughing it up, goofing off and breaking rules. He believes that doing well in school is *"for sissies,"* an embarrassing and adolescent term that he uses with Nino when he is sure Marge isn't within earshot.

It is so not what a young boy deserves.

It doesn't take Nino long to realize that the only thing he and his father have in common is their competing desire to please Marge, which he knows to be something with which his dad sometimes struggles. So to his credit, in a display of confidence beyond his ten years, Nino proves every bit an equal when he devises a strategy to take himself out of his father's crosshairs. It would also deliver on an unspoken promise to please Marge in a way Tony never could. He accomplishes it all by saying four words every mother in the neighborhood prays to hear. "*I have a vocation,*" Nino tells them, on the night he announces his calling to the priesthood. It's 1960 and in three years, he will be old enough to move away. Upon finishing eighth grade, he tells them, he will start living full-time at Sacred Heart Seminary.

As he knew it would, his big announcement makes Marge forever grateful. Like Catholic moms the world over, she holds to a belief that she might earn "*a special indulgence*" to gain entry to Heaven if she raises a son who becomes a priest. With that, Marge bestows much pride on her oldest male offspring, who is by far the most sensitive and vulnerable of her three boys.

I'm the one in the middle. Blessed with a fair bit of hand-eye coordination and a passion for sports, I am growing up with hometown idols like *Rocky*, *Blinkie* and *Fats*, in the persons of Rocky Colavito, Gordie Howe and Alex Delvecchio—as well as Toronto center, Davey Keon. My allegiance to a Leaf is because of Foster Hewitt on Saturday nights, which I never miss. His hurried refrain, *"He shoots...he scores!"* is echoed twenty times for Davey during his rookie season. Toronto's Number 14 was also a former Mass server, according to a feature I read in *Catholic Boy Magazine* when I was eight. *CONFITEOR DEO OMNIPOTENTI! DAVEEEE!* I scream every time he touches the puck. God am I a dweeb. Oh well. One of the best two-way players in the game, my *Hockey Night in Canada* hero would go on to prove time and again he had jets when he set an NHL record with eight short-handed goals in a single season.

ET CUM SPIRITU TUO...Daveeeeee!

No surprise. I join every team I can, which Marge and Tony encourage since it keeps me out of trouble. Consumed by Little League baseball and pond hockey, I would soon add grade school football and basketball to the mix as a starter in every sport.

Determined to please my dad, in predictable fashion my academic career begins without distinction. Big mistake. *Thwaaack*. My first end-of-year report card earns a serious lambasting from Marge, who is as much fun as a nun during Stations of the Cross when she whacks me for not trying. *Lesson learned, Ma. Lesson Learned.* Given my dad's hectic schedule, nothing I do catches his attention anyway. So like Kathy and Nino before me, I fall in line, since there is nothing I hate more in this world than getting lambasted.

Owing to birth order, we match up like peanut butter and jelly on warm toast, Marge and me. Blessed with reasonable instincts and eager to please, I fast assume the role of a wide-eyed puppy, ever faithful by her side. I swear, sometimes she looks at me like she can *hear* my tail wagging.

I'm a preschooler when Marge begins sharing stories about days gone by, back when she first met our dad. And even though I remain every bit a clueless innocent, she has a way of confiding in me like she is talking to a friend. Before long, she would begin sharing opinions about everything with me—from spiritual matters to current events to books she is reading—none of which I am old enough to grasp. The fact that it all sails over my head matters not one bit to Marge, however. Whenever she talks to me like I am all grown up, she takes as much delight in my bewildered looks as she does sharing her stories and insights. No one could have predicted where it all would lead.

Baptized *Patrick Jerome*, the baby of our family is eight years Kathy's junior. Blessed with an effervescent spirit, he is the smartest of the bunch by far, in my estimation. Tony and Marge love their little one to pieces even though he proves to be more of a handful than the rest of us. Plagued by a stammer as a youngster, Patrick gets away with behavior that would never be tolerated if exhibited by his siblings.

"*Puh...puh...please, can I carry the cuh-cake? Puh-please. I won't drop it. I puh-puh-promise, Mom.*"

After coaxing from Tony, Marge concedes.

Suspicious, but not yet aware of the true depths of young Patrick's antics, she cautions him, "*Carry it slowly, honey, while we sing for Mikee.*"

Lights out. He circles the kitchen. At the sink, he flips each glowing candle into the suds. Turning, he feigns a stumble as he deposits that buttercream beauty flush onto my lap. Our dad, the man-boy, claps with glee. *"Brutal! Woohoo!"* Lights on. Marge has to slap Tony on his shoulder to contain him. Frosting and crushed nuts cover my body. I figure it a blessing that he didn't light me on fire as I survey the cake crumbs all over the floor. Tony can't stop laughing. He loves nothing more than watching his youngest engage in displays of heartless hijinks. And Patrick never fails to deliver. So that's how those two roll, with mutual admiration. Growing up as the baby in his own family, Tony will be allies forever with Patrick. The true strength of their bond would reveal itself in earnest a few short years later when they would become involved in a dubious collaboration known to Marge but to no one else. Considering the stakes, it should have come as no surprise.

I am a twenty-month-old toddler, Kathy is in second grade and Nino is just beginning kindergarten when Marge arrives home with her newborn Patrick to announce that it's time for a family overhaul. Tony is frustrated in his dead-end job at the hotel. Verbal rants have become common. With alcohol fueling his rage, Marge knows it is just a matter of time before his outbursts escalate. She corners him one morning as he holds open the fridge, staring into the void. "We're going to give up the drink, Tony. Together, you and me, we are going to get sober. You will concentrate on your job. And you will never raise a hand to these children. Do you hear me? I will be in charge of that. In fact, if this is gonna work, you will have to take a backseat on parenting altogether. There can be but one boss of these kids, and you're looking at her. Agreed?"

Even with that, Tony cannot see what he has become. Truth is he can't even count the bottles of Labatts standing tall inside the fridge. With no memory about what happened the night before, he is helpless to argue. So he appeases. He tells the love of his life the words she needs to hear, hoping they will buy him time. Besides, his head feels like someone has planted an axe in it. "Fine, fine dear...we'll stop drinking and you will handle the children. I got it...enough already. Really. I'll just focus on work. I'll stay out of your way as far as the kids go. Okay? How does that sound, darling?"

Staying out of the way will not be a problem. That he can handle. Sobriety, on the other hand, will present a different kind of challenge, he knows.

He seals their deal with a hug.

Steadfast, Marge's example keeps Tony off the drink.

A new chapter unfolds.

Sober for the first time in his adult life, Tony finds his culinary skills improve, as does his reputation. It's not long before he is hired away from his dead-end job at the hotel kitchen to begin cooking for the Executive Dining Room of a prestigious downtown advertising agency. It makes Marge proud to know they have a plan that is coming together. "Good man, Tony, you're a good man. Now, just bring home those paychecks of yours to me and we'll all be fine."

Meanwhile, Marge carries on, happy in their arrangement.

Like most other moms in the neighborhood, she spends her days cleaning the house. She also launders and irons school uniforms. She shops. She cooks. She pays bills. She organizes excursions downtown to the David Whitney Building for our medical checkups and vaccinations. She also commandeers shoe-shopping outings to an upscale menswear store, where she befriends a somewhat nervous salesman by the name of Leon. "I'm paying Mr. Hughes and Mr. Hatcher a premium for your expertise here, pal. I'm watching you. Take your time. Fit 'em right," Marge warns.

Poor guy.

Regular back-to-school shopping happens at a store called *Federals*, not far from where Marge's mom and dad live, so we stop in to visit our grandparents often.

Back in our neighborhood, she organizes homework time. She also attends all of our dance recitals, plays, religious pageants and even a few sporting events. There is never any doubt that she loves us each for who we are. She also reminds us often how much our dad loves us too, which is good, since he is not home much, and when he is, he never says it.

In Marge's world, ridicule is out. Positive reinforcement is in. She also makes sure that we understand that we each have our own jobs to do, just as she has hers. Respect for her and for our dad, as well as for each other, comes with the territory — unless we want to get *"knocked into next Tuesday."*

For that, I would become her prime example.

Set in her ways, Marge never learned to drive so she never got a license. She prefers walking, or riding the city bus with a good book, traditions she had established as a girl, which makes running errands with her an ordeal and a half.

"When will the bus be here, Mom, when will it be here? How much longer do we have to wait? How much longer?" I whine.

"Hey. Keep your pants on, buddy. The bus will come into sight as soon as that man waiting with us lights his cigarette. Watch. You'll see."

Huh?

Click goes the Zippo. She cuffs my arm as the bus comes into view while the man takes the first pull on his smoke. Talk about spooky.

Nannah-Nannah — Nannah-Nannah....

It was around the time that I discovered that featherless dead birdie on the floor of our garage that Marge began confiding about her lifestyle back when she was pregnant with Patrick. "I'm going to tell you a secret, Mikee. Alcohol had taken over our lives. There was nothing casual about it. The drink was either going to kill us or we were going to kill each other. Of course, we couldn't risk that since we had a beautiful family to raise."

I'm staring at a colander of peeled potatoes on the counter next to the sink. Lost to it all, I nod in blank agreement. I'm obsessed wondering if the ants are still out there marching around the concrete, searching for traces of dead birdie splatter.

"You don't have a clue what I just told you, do you?" She reads me.

"Mmm...nope...not really, Mom."

"Come over here, my little sparrow. Your mother needs some love."

She thanks me with a big hug for being a good listener. A quiet whisper and a kiss to the top of my head follow. "Aren't you a beautiful boy? I bet you're soaking it all in, aren't you?"

Huh?

She slaps my fanny.

"You're a good one, Mikee. Now, get outta my sight until dinner."

SEVEN

NO STANDING

In honor of my fifth year, Marge arranges for two of the finest girls in the neighborhood to take turns walking me down to the far west-end of their high school to deliver me to kindergarten. The devil in me has me all but convinced that they are my girlfriends as we stroll hand in hand every Monday, Wednesday and Friday morning, just like we're heading out on a date. Can you imagine? Such a little goofball I am, loving life in the *MikeeZone*, about to take my first flight. It's a blustery October afternoon.

Kathy and Nino have just arrived home. Since it's the end of their school week, they join me in the living room for a bit of TV time. Kathy takes charge. Marge is busy preparing a feast for her three-year-old, Patrick, who is occupying himself spinning in an aluminum bowl on the linoleum.

Compulsive on Fridays, Marge has spent her entire day cleaning, made evident by the intoxicating tang of Pine-Sol and Comet that wafts from the kitchen. It's a full-combo assault in the living room where we sit as a holy trinity of aromatics has my head spinning. Surrounded by scents of Murphy's Oil Soap, Pledge and Windex, I'm counting the waves of vacuum tracks on the carpet when a voice on TV beckons.

"The Mouse Cartoon for today is…"

A title appears on the screen. Without thinking, I mumble three words before Mousketeer Karen can say it. Then Kathy screams three words of her own. "Mikee can read! Mikee can read!"

Holy Howdy Doody Time!

I had no idea.

Nino shushes us both.

Moments later, I high-step it out of there when I decide that it's as good a time as any to run away from home.

I am not mad at anybody or upset about anything. I am just feeling confident and headstrong, traits that I had no doubt picked up from Marge by example. In my little head, I am one of *The Little Rascals*, living proof that television influences behavior. I'm just doing what Spanky or Froggy or Stymie would do any day of the week, when I load a few belongings into a handkerchief, tie the corners to a broken broomstick, and slip away. My memory of that day is as vivid as one of those old *Our Gang* episodes.

It's a steel-gray day. Heading toward the high school, I see bushels of damp debris burning at curbside. Musty smoke is swirling over rooftops. Gusts of wind catch screen doors by surprise. Fence gates open and close like metronomes keeping time to the glut of accordion lessons that are infecting our neighborhood like an epidemic. The one thing lacking for my little journey is a terrific doggie like *Petey,* to keep me company and protect me. He's the *real* star of that Little Rascals program, after all. Every time that funny-looking creature appears, I want to crawl inside our Magnavox to give him a big hug.

At the end of the block I spot a street sign. *"Cathedral."* I can't even pronounce it. A moment later, I find myself on the receiving end of a message from above that I can read.

Kathy is quick to find me. I'm sitting on a curb. Obedient, I'm observing the sign hanging over my head.

"No Standing."

Go figure.

We hold hands walking home. Before I know it, we are on the concrete driveway that leads to the side door of our house. It feels good to be back on the old launch pad where young Patrick would venture out on his own a few short years later.

He is six when he takes control of an ice cream-wagon-tricycle. It's a hand-me-down from Nino, who had spent his years as a toddler within the safe confines of the slab running along the side of our house, pretending to sell frozen treats to imaginary patrons. When our *Little Mr. Hijinks* takes command of that pedal wagon, however, he puts it to a different use altogether.

He stuffs an old bed sheet, a comb and a pair of scissors inside his little compartment before setting out on a self-ordained mission. Patrick's goal is to snare unsuspecting prey so he can give them something that he calls "*surprise haircuts.*" His efforts are met with complete disappointment until he has a revelation.

Along with his tools of the trade, he puts an empty bowl and a jug of water in his cubby. Riding up and down the sidewalk, he jingles his little bell. Whenever he spots a potential customer, he delivers his pitch up-close, with a smile, an approving nod and a half-whisper. *"Hey, your duh-doggie looks thirsty. Wanna give him a duh-duh- drink?"* Whenever a little boy stops to take him up on the offer, young Pat, who is big for his age, pours some water into the bowl to occupy the animal, before throwing a sheet around his surprised customer's shoulders to begin recklessly snipping away.

Irate parents from all around the block are soon lining up at our front door to complain to Marge, who knows all too well that her youngest is not just unskilled as a barber, but he is merciless.

So there you have it. A nuclear family of the Sixties. The youngest is brimming with mischief, which brings utter delight to his man-boy father, who's spending most of his time working or recreating. I focus on sports and try to do just well enough in school to avoid my mom's wrath. The oldest boy and namesake competes with his dad to please his mom in a way his father never could when he becomes his mother's ticket to Heaven. And then there is the first-born, an absolute angel if ever there was one.

As for Marge, one has to wonder how she developed such inspired confidence to give us each the courage to accept our fates. Time-honored traditions help. She has faith in God. She believes in her Church. She loves her country. In fact, she has lately begun humming, *"Hail to the Chief,"* to celebrate the election of our first Irish Catholic President. She also trusts that her Westside neighborhood is a perfect place to raise her young family.

So far, so good.

God willing, the nightmare that began this little saga will turn out to be just some twisted dream. *Phew.* Thank God. I'm feeling better already.

Much better.

EIGHT

FAUST

Detroit's Eight Mile is due north beyond streets with names like Fenkell and McNichol, which everyone knows to be Five and Six Mile Roads. Anchoring our neighborhood to the south, Joy Road would be *One Mile* by the markers on the freeway. But no one calls it that. It's just *Joy*, which means *Hallelujah* to my mom and me, since it has a regular city bus service running into the heart of downtown, via Clairmount, with no need to transfer. We live a half-mile north of Joy, off West Chicago, on a street with a diabolical name. It refers to some old German myth, about which no one ever speaks. When I looked it up, I learned that that ancient legend had something to do with some guy who made a bargain with the Devil. He must have been real desperate is all I can figure.

Faust borders the eastern edge of *Stein*; a flat, grassy thirty-acre playfield named to honor a local judge, but everyone calls it *Cody* for the high school at the end of our street. Except for a medical clinic and a dentist's office one house from ours, our stretch, which runs north-south, is the exclusive domain of two-story homes, all covered in red face-brick, aligned in a perfect row. Except for alternating roof-pitches, every house is identical, right down to the small concrete porch stoops, the honey-colored stain on the cupboards, and the style of sheet linoleum that lines the floors of each kitchen. The only thing that differs is the quality of the sound from radios on window sills or atop workbenches in each garage, which blare whenever the Tigers or Lions or Wings are playing.

Populated with laborers and city workers, our block is also home to a handful of professionals like the doctor who lives a few houses down who works at a hospital called *Henry Ford*, where I was born. Blue-collar or white coat makes no difference on our street, however. If your dad goes to work every day, you are working class by the standards of our neighborhood. And there's not a lick of shame in that. Not in our proud city.

None whatsoever.

An advertising executive lives over the fence to the south. Just like *Dennis the Menace,* I had my very own Mr. Wilson right next door. A terrific father of three, his wife Bunny works as an RN at Grace Hospital, where The Great Harry Houdini met his maker the year the Belcrest opened. Wil, as he is known to his friends, works downtown in a 38-story building called *The Book Tower,* which means he has to drive into the sun to and from work. Such is the plight of Westsiders who are nine-to-fivers. The dad beyond our other fence is married to Libby. A lifelong member of the League of Women Voters, she volunteers to work the polls every Election Day. Otherwise she works full-time as a mom. He is an automotive engineer at *The Proving Grounds* in nearby Dearborn. A proud father of four, he has two sons who are *Explorers,* about which I am clueless. I never even became a Cub Scout, so I wouldn't know. Between school and sports, plus a few Saturday chores, I spend all my time memorizing the Latin Mass with hopes of making Marge proud by becoming the youngest altar boy in parish history. Truth be known, she's scaring me into it. She tells me that the quicker I become a Mass server, the better my chances are that I might get into heaven *"when the big one hits."*

Huh?

Matters of eternal salvation aside, it doesn't take me long to figure out that I might be able to make some easy money serving weddings once I learn the Latin. That would be a real boon since Marge squeaks when it comes to laying down cash for allowances. Except for doling out some haircut money and a couple of bucks for a cheeseburger and a half-order of fries every few weeks at a lunch counter called *Sky's*, Marge has mastered the art of non-monetary rewards. "*Come here, Mikee. Take this. I need you to wipe down each and every slat of that venetian blind over there*," she says as she dips an old cloth diaper in a bucket of Pine-Sol. "*Do a good job and I'll let you watch a movie with me later. Half-ass it and you'll be scrubbin' the toilet.*"

When she puts it that way, I'm happy to oblige.

Fact is that getting a skimpy allowance for doing chores is the least of my worries at this moment. There is a missile crisis looming concerning somewhere called Cuba. *Soviet boogiemen* are out there. Dads all over the block are talking about "*the bomb.*" Test blares from civil defense sirens are all too common. Word on the street is that the situation is "getting serious." Best I can tell the escalation of chatter has something to do with pigs floating in a bay, or some such thing. I try to imagine a sea of bloated oinkers bobbing up and down; washing up on some shore. Nothing is making sense. With the press of a button, they tell us our lives could be over in a blinding white flash.

All over the block, families are doing whatever they can to prepare. In fact, Mr. Wilson let it be known that he has just signed a contract for a little construction project over our side-yard fence. Eight-year-old Patrick and I are pressing up against the chain-link on our backyard driveway when backhoes move in to start excavation for the fallout shelter next-door.

"Excuse me. Am I muh-missing something here, muh-Mikee? Do they know suh-sumpthin' we don't?" he presses. "What's our puh-plan? We *do* have a plan, don't we?"

I have no idea what to say.

Patrick shows no patience for the pause.

"I guh-guess that muh-means we're *uh-uck -fayed*, duh-don't it?"

God love him.

I would soon come to know everything about that concrete bunker next door, since I played inside it with my buddy Lee almost every day. It was fun at first. Then we started pretending that we were waiting for radioactive winds to stop blowing and for the sun to shine again. It got really creepy when I took note of how it was stocked. There where blankets and bedding and a gazillion jugs of bottled water down there. There were shelves full of canned goods. There were radios and flashlights and lanterns and spare batteries, and a gas generator, the size of a small refrigerator. They even had a chessboard and stacks of board games like *Parcheesi* and *Sorry*. Boy, were they ready.

Us, not so much.

Back on our side of the fence, *being ready* means going to confession *twice* a week and attending Mass more often. That's about it. No fallout shelter for us. Believing the adage that "*The family that prays together stays together*," sometimes we even say the Rosary before bedtime, joining in prayer with Bishop Fulton Sheen, with whom Marge has grown smitten. She keeps it simple. For her, it is all about earning graces and storing them up to make sure we all get into heaven *together* when, *not if*, the big one hits.

Everyone knows. It's just a matter of time.

Meanwhile, Friday night traditions continue. It's bowling league for Tony with young Patrick in tow. Kathy and Nino attend dances or sleepovers. That leaves Marge and me alone to watch her freakazoid fables on the tube when I get home from hockey.

Even with the Police Commissioner of the fifth largest city in America living down the block, no one feels safe. His home faces the high school. It's the one with the "*No Standing*" sign in front of it. That should have been enough of a tip-off as to his status as a genuine public figure, although few kids gave the Commissioner his due. By the standards of our neighborhood, a "*celebrity dad*" is the one who paints the beer ads on the centerfield scoreboard at Tiger Stadium; or the one who touts himself to be a "*film distributor*." That one acts like he is some sort of Hollywood mogul. Truth be known, his primary distribution route has him sipping beers while stocking peep shows at downtown clubs like *The Empress*, or at strip joints out near the airport, about which his sons brag to no end.

A block east of Faust is a supermarket where Kathy begins working on the day she turns sixteen. Next to that is Cody Pharmacy, home to an eight-seat soda counter best known for a concoction called a *Graveyard* because it's guaranteed to make you feel like death if you drink one. A despicable "dare-magnet," it's a mix of chocolate syrup, tomato juice, *Nehi* Grape and God knows what else. A small sign on the counter advises: *"Graveyards are available for take-out only."* No thank you.

Behind the fountain, high on the wall over the mirrors and stacks of tall glasses, are framed photos of my baseball teams. They've earned such prominent placement because of the tireless efforts of our league's founder, a lawyer who lives down the street. In a neighborhood where the term *"family summer vacation"* is an absolute oxymoron for most, Mr. John Hubacher came to our rescue. Like Spencer Tracy's Father Flanagan, from the movie *Boys Town,* Mr. H even gave our league a motto. *"Better Boys through Better Baseball"* became the mission statement of The Barney McCosky League, which was named after a local hero whose playing career ended before I was born.

Every kid knew the stats of our league's namesake. Barney hit over .300 in six of his first seven seasons in the bigs. In the 1940s, he trailed only Hall of Famers Hank Greenberg and Charlie Gehringer in batting average among Tiger starters. After eleven seasons, he ended his major league career with a.312 batting average and a .984 fielding percentage. When his playing days were over, Barney came home to the neighborhood to own and operate something that Detroiters call a *"party store."* Located on Joy Road, his *one-stop* was a place where customers could pick up essentials like bags of ice, packs of smokes, along with beer, wine and booze.

Our league required a tryout, followed by a draft, which proved to be the most exciting day of the year for a kid like me whose dad could never find time to play catch. On that spring morning every year, hundreds of kids would strut their stuff with big numbers pinned to their shirts, as an army of clipboard-toting coaches stood at attention on the foul lines to bandy about descriptives like *"scrappy"* and *"gamer."*

I was one of the lucky ones. Each draft day became a rite of passage for me, though plenty of boys didn't make the cut. The *unchosen* just had to deal with it, which must have been hard for those few handfuls of dads who made time to show up for tryouts to support their young sons. In a neighborhood devoid of coddling, there was no means of appeal. Not in our baseball league. Either you made it on own merits or you didn't march in the big parade that kicked-off each season behind a slow-moving car with loudspeakers mounted to its roof.

We would assemble in mothball-reeking uniformed splendor on a street called Plainview before stepping down the middle of Joy to the sound of a scratchy John Phillip Souza record, thanks to a *Philco* turntable balanced shotgun on the lead station wagon's bench seat. The music would change to the National Anthem as soon as we landed in the middle of Cody. That's when neighbors would stop sweeping their walks. With music bouncing off all sixty homes surrounding the field, everyone within earshot would stand at attention. In a nod to our league's namesake, Tiger greats like Rocky Colavito and Stormin' Norman Cash would join our neighbors at the start of each season to cover their hearts, as well.

I love my neighborhood for that memory.

Catholic, Protestant, Baptist, Methodist, Greaser, Frat, Shark or Jet, it made no difference. In uniform, we were all just ballplayers dreaming of glory. While no one could mistake our surroundings for pretty, we were a pride-filled and dedicated bunch, especially when it came to baseball.

Heading west from the Southfield Freeway, a fungal blight had wiped out too many elms in the 1950s, giving unintended prominence to telephone poles and light standards that line the ways. They illuminate concrete streets and strips of sidewalks and small lawns that front rows of houses that defy developer-crafted descriptives. Devoid of home-styles like *Tudor, Queen Anne* or *Mediterranean Revival*, the majority of houses in our Parish are nondescript one-and-a-half story wood frame and brick bungalow affairs. Most have dormers with converted attics. Some have siding made of a space-age material called *asbestos*. Eaves and windowsills are trimmed with arrays of lead-based paints.

From our concrete driveway, Cody Field appears as a magnificent multi-function fitness complex to me. In reality, it's nothing but a barebones, 30-acre city-mowed parcel, home to four chain-link backstops, a drinking fountain, and a football field where the high school plays its home games and the marching band practices every mid-morning in the fall, making drumbeats bounce off every surrounding house. Midfield on Cathedral, a well-placed hydrant floods a patch of grass for hockey, which becomes my home away from home in winter during my early days of grade school. A nearby streetlight allows us to play pick-up games on Fridays, late into the evening.

As for trees, a solitary heavy-limbed oak stands proud in the middle of our field. The only specimen of its kind for miles, even the blight that took so many Dutch Elms couldn't deter homecoming bonfire celebrations from happening out there under its branches. Each fall and winter, pep squads would nourish its enormous trunk with gasoline before dropping a match to light it ablaze. If not for the responsiveness of our neighborhood firefighters, that proud tree would surely have perished. But like most of the people who lived nearby, adversity served a purpose in making our old oak even stronger.

Beyond the high school, on Joy, sits The Thomas A. Edison branch of the Detroit Public Library system, where I discovered girls gathered after school, which made me something of an academic at an early age. My own little slice of Nirvana revealed, homework did not seem a bit burdensome there, far from the obsessive behavior of the fanatical nuns at our grade school.

Just east of the library stands our neighborhood fire station, known as *Engine Company No. 55* and *Ladder Company No. 27*. It hosts an Open House every summer. That's where eight-year-olds like me can show up unattended to inspect the shiny equipment. Some kids come to climb on the trucks. Some come to slide down the fire pole. I come longing to experience something that I discovered quite by accident the summer before.

It changed my life forever.

Patrick is on his knees. Cornered by a porch railing, he is pleading with a massive German shepherd. Hands clasped, with his fingers pointing toward Heaven, his words are running together. "*Puh-puh-please-don't-eat-me-muh-muh-Missy-puh-please-duh-don't-eat-me,*" he begs. My slow approach allows him to get up and back away as the guard dog turns its attention to me. This is a first. I had never before been alone with a dog, not to mention one bred to protect and serve.

Fangs glisten and eyes sparkle. A drip of saliva makes this beast look like a glutton in need of a few more bites of lunch.

Then it happened.

It started with unwavering eye contact, followed by a slight head-tilt and a magnificent wag of its tail. Three sticky licks cover my face.

Cue the spine-tingling splendor.

That's when I knew I was hooked and that I would forever be in search of that glorious sensation of connection that happens when boy first meets dog.

That's what drew me to our fire station that late summer morning. Eye contact and a tail wag was all I was after. I didn't even need to pet the darn thing. Soon after my arrival, however, I realized that neither Dalmatians nor any other kind of canine mascot was standard issue at our neighborhood firehouse, best known for its civil defense siren atop its roof. At the stroke of one, it blasted on the first Saturday of every month with such regularity that neighbors set kitchen clocks by it. For Marge, the sound of that siren became just one more reminder to heed the three words in black block letters on the big white sign near the freeway back in October of '62:

"PRAY FOR PEACE."

Despite on-going threats of nuclear annihilation, nothing could keep us from our appointed rounds on Halloween. In a neighborhood bursting with elementary school-age baby boomers, the strength of our numbers proved too much for sidewalks to handle. Negotiating storm drains close to the curb became the simplest way to cover ground when you were in a candy-collecting competition with your little brother whose resolve is fierce. Fearing his bounty would bust through his bag, Patrick became the first kid on our block to drag a pillowcase up and down our porch-lit street, where pumpkins greeted us on every stoop.

Ours stood out. Hand-painted by a commercial artist from the ad agency, it was embellished with goodies from our dad's walk-in. Red pepper halves for ears. A yellow zucchini nose. Cucumber slices and olives for eyes and raisins for freckles became standard fare.

His thoughtfulness pleased Marge to no end.

Strolling down our little walk to stand in front of the house with hands on her hips, she smiles broadly to admire our dad's artful offering, which sits on the corner of our small front porch as ghosts and goblins begin lining the street.

Dressed to look like a forlorn little hobo, Patrick comes up behind her. "BOOOOOOOO!"

A foot off the ground she jumps.

"Gotcha, Mom. I gotcha!" Pat boasts.

"Oh, Patrick. Come here, you little sneak," she hollers as she grabs him for a hug and a tickle.

The next morning brings a sleepy cheer.

"Woo-hoo-for-Holy Days!"

The first of November means no school for us Catholics. Thank you, Lord.

Nino is already gone. He is serving Mass on this Feast of All Saints. Dutiful, Marge attends. Apparently, there are special graces to be earned by going to church on a Holy Day.

Patrick and I are content to be lining our candy end-to-end on our bedroom floor to see whose *train* is longest. Winner takes all. As always, it results in a smackdown. With Kathy occupied in the kitchen making breakfast, we mimic classic TV battles of wrestlers with names like *Bobo Brazil*, *Dick the Bruiser*, and *Fritz von Erich*, famous for his "*iron claw hold*," which is my go-to move whenever I can get Pat on his little back.

Putting aside our candy for a moment, we configure our beds and a dresser into a makeshift *death cage*. Introductions begin. Standing proud in the middle, Pat clutches one of our dad's bowling trophies as a microphone to proclaim himself *The Patron Saint of Ireland* and me *The Archangel Michael* before our little head bashing begins. As temporary members of an elite fraternity known to most mortals as *The Communion of Saints*, we delight in pounding the daylights out of each other whenever no one is around to stop us. At battle's end, bloody and bruised, those skirmishes remain between ourselves. No crying. No grousing. No hard feelings. We considered that our version of brotherly love. Besides, we were both mindful that Marge would be walking through the front door any minute. Whining would earn us a real licking.

She always greets us in the same exact fashion. As long as our skulls aren't crushed-in and our teeth are intact, she ignores every bash and bloodstain when we roll down the stairs. "Hi, guys....whoa...looks like you've been having some fun." She laughs. "Thanks for behaving for your sister. I prayed for you at Mass, boys. Oooh, doesn't the house smell good. Let's all have some breakfast, shall we?" Big hugs follow.

Our neighborhood extends from Joy to a few blocks north of Plymouth. East to West, it runs from the Southfield Freeway to a tree-covered recreation area called Rouge.

Larger but much less grand than New York's Central Park, Rouge has an 18-hole golf course, picnic areas, cross-country running trails and some ball fields. It's also home to *Brennan Pool.* Olympic-size, it features a ten-meter diving platform, from which I would never dare to tempt fate by jumping. No way. God forbid a gust should come up. Urban legend had it that one boy went splat on the concrete surround when a burst of wind caught him while diving from thirty-feet above.

In winter, ice-covered wood-track toboggan runs hover over a parking area next to a ten-acre city hydrant-flooded meadow. That's where hockey-skating near-teen boys and figure skating girls enjoy cold evenings together. It's an ideal venue for first dates. In our neighborhood, holding a girl's hand while you're skating on the pond at Rouge means you like her. Sharing a ten-cent cup of watery hot chocolate with her in front of your buddies, surrounded by a sea of stinky shoes in a beat-up warming trailer, means you're on a date. It works for me.

It's a neighborhood where every dad has at least one job and where parents often end conversations with the words *"no guts, no glory."* And kids learn the meaning of the word *gamble* long before they are old enough to have money in their pockets, by playing a card game called *bloody knuckles*. It's a neighborhood where families walk to church and when your mom needs you, she just stands on the front porch and screams like a banshee. *"Do not make me yell for you,"* becomes every mother's mantra. Abject embarrassment causes most kids to head home on school nights when they hear a subtle siren drone. On Faust, the streetlights buzz just before they light up.

As in most Detroit neighborhoods, dads drive the family car to work, so home deliveries lighten moms' loads. Uniformed truck drivers with pencils stuck under their hats drive step vans loaded with baked goods from *Awrey's*. Yellow and green milk trucks carry dairy products from *Twin Pines*. Other trucks carry big tins of potato chips and round cardboard containers of laundry detergent to each house. Milk-chutes built door handle-high just to the left of every side door on our block allow for *"worry-free home delivery."*

At a time when boys pay more attention to the shine of a baby moon hubcap than they do their girlfriends, everyone knows the meaning of the word *changeover* since every job in town relates in some way to the auto industry. An all too brief hiatus, changeover gives assembly-liners a respite to allow factories time to re-tool for the new model year. On our block, kids as young as eight can identify the make, model and year of any vehicle on the street by gazing only at taillight configurations.

"Call it, Jerry," I challenge.

"Sixty-one Dart, 3-speed-push-button on the dash. Slant six, I'm bettin'."

"Geeez. Sorry I asked. No blood. Good call."

For my friend Jerry's sake, it's too bad the nuns don't give pop quizzes on such matters.

Around Labor Day tandem trucks begin to roll. In keeping with strict tradition set by *The Big Three*, dealerships in our neighborhood surround those precious, first-in-the-nation arrivals with tall canvas fencing. High intrigue. It's all very hush-hush. New models are supposed to remain under wraps until a programmed *Premier Event*. Excitement builds when searchlights appear on each car lot to rake the night sky. For some, tracking a beam to its source is like finding a pot of gold at the end of a rainbow.

Our beam tracker-in-chief is a budding young artist. Twelve-year-old Eddie O'Malley, a classmate of Nino's at St. Suzanne, has become known for his spot-on caricatures of nuns at our school. So funny. He is also gaining notoriety for his ability to impart *personality* to renderings of cars by utilizing an ingenious medium. He draws on paper plates, the kind with crinkled edges that you can pinch from a cupboard without notice.

Stuffing his nylon warm-up with colored pencils, he finds a perch atop one of the 4x4 posts supporting the dealership's canvas surround. Determined to earn a few days of popularity at school, he balances as he delineates every new model taillight, grille, bumper and fin before being whisked away by security. Always ready to trade one of his drawings for a few nickel-cartons of chocolate milk, through his exploits he exemplifies a confident, harmless exuberance that makes a kid like me proud to know him.

Harmless adventures aside, like in any city neighborhood the world-over, a moment of high drama could turn a day ugly in an instant, just as it did on a sad Sunday morning when I learned the meaning of the word *ironic*. Sometime during the night before, a wonderful mom who lives a few doors from our church hid away in a bathroom of her home, where she locked the door from the inside and set it ablaze. It resulted in a rare closed-casket wake for the wife of a City of Detroit Fire Captain whose kids were among my best friends.

The weekend before, I had spent an hour visiting with their mom in her kitchen. Just the two of us. I played with their dog, a magnificent boxer named Duke, as she stood by the sink, cloth-drying her dishes, talking non-stop and laughing. Such a terrific laugh it was. It wasn't until her passing that I began to understand that things are not always as they seem.

Irony paid another visit a few weeks later.

It was a Friday evening when the son of a prominent neighbor died in a car crash around the corner. That boy had been drag racing behind Kathy's store on a strip of street called Fitzpatrick that is lined with heavy wooden telephone poles and steel light standards. It fronts a row of small tool & die shops that border an abutment of rocky embankment where railroad tracks block cross traffic for a perfect quarter mile. In the days before seatbelts, even the teenage son of Detroit's Police Commissioner could perish racing a street-rod on bald tires with poor suspension. God rest his soul.

It's a neighborhood teeming with taunting and the culture is grounded in boasting, which often results in stupid dares, about which Marge knew a thing or two. Seeing a few arm and leg prostheses lined-up outside the shower room on open swim nights down the block at Cody's indoor pool was enough evidence for me as to the price some kids pay for bragging or accepting stupid dares. Seeing those fake appendages was all it took for most kids to figure out that losing a limb for jumping a train was no bargain. With all of this, I had to thank my lucky stars that my family could avoid such drama.

For us, it is smooth sailing in the heart of Detroit 28, where life is an absolute breeze.

NINE

THE DOMINICANS

From Faust to the edge of Rouge Park, the small campus of St. Suzanne sits smack in the middle, eight blocks west. Home to our elementary school and to the church where we worship, it anchors our universe. Surrounded by single-story homes and a smattering of co-op apartments on our end, the school and church make up the heart of a parish that touches the lives of 1,600 families.

A residential street separates our church from the rectory where the priests live. All God-fearing good men, there isn't a hint of deviant behavior among them, thank God. Nearby, a convent houses thirty nuns, all *Sisters of the Order of St. Dominic.* Founded in the year 1216 somewhere in France, the sisters of our Dominican Order were best known for having eyes in the back of their heads since there were a thousand kids shoehorned into twenty-four classrooms.

Nuns-in-training, known as *"Novitiates,"* were taught never to show weakness by elder Sisters who impose marine-like disciplinary measures, which they enforce with varying degrees of reprimand. On the spot and without warning they make girls drop to their knees in the middle of hallways to check the length of their skirts. For boys, they whack metal-edged rulers on wooden desktops, rap knuckles or cuff the back of heads. Major indiscretions like pitching pennies or talking to girls during recess earn a furious yardstick wave as they dispatch you to the principal's office.

Like an eager covey of quail, a wide-eyed nun patrol paces a buffer that separates two playgrounds. Closed to traffic during school hours, a quiet street called Westwood forms a demilitarized zone, of sorts. On one side is an oasis of navy-and-white civility, where uniformed girls engage in polite conversation and genteel games like hopscotch and jump rope. On our playground, mayhem reigns. Clots of boys in dress shirts and ties run roughshod, some in torn and bloodied clothes, a predictable reaction to the confining rules of behavior that dominate our lives. With threats of holy war for breaches of gender segregation, boys earn close scrutiny, except when we're in our church basement, of course. That's where we perfect the *"shuffle-ball change."* It's also where we wait out storms.

Tradition allows boys and girls to be together down there, below our church, for tap rehearsals in preparation for *The Annual St. Suzanne Dance Recital*, which every parent attends. The second exception has to do with tornado warnings. Sitting on the cold linoleum, boys and girls huddle together in a dark southwest corner, holding hands, passing notes — and God forbid making eye contact — until storms blow over or warnings pass. Given the nuns' obsession with keeping the girls to themselves on the playgrounds, no one should have been surprised to learn that the boys at our school pray for tornado warnings more than most kids pray for snow days. Scary storms set our hearts a flutter.

We also do a mean *dig-step*…tap…tap.

TEN

HAVE FAITH

St. Suzanne Parish became established in 1946, the year after Marge's conversion to Catholicism, an event that threatened to turn her world upside-down as she prepared for her marriage to Tony.

"How hard can this be?" She cannot stop her mind from racing. *"Come on, Margaret. Get hold of yourself. You can do this."*

"Can't I?" she wonders.

Were it not for her reflection in the mirror on top of her dresser, she might have had even more reason for doubt. Standing tall on tiptoe, she admires her profile with a lengthy side-glance, grateful that the young beauty looking back at her is a picture of calming support. It's just the encouragement she needs.

"Oh, you! What are you fretting over, girl? You'll be fine."

Attentive to fashion but no slave to it, young Marge is on her way to meet a priest for her first day of religious instruction. She ties a soft silk scarf around her neck before fussing with her matching pale yellow cardigan and flattening the front of her mid-calf skirt. *"There we go. That should do it."* Running out the door, she throws a lightweight raincoat over her shoulders. It flows to her ankles. She wears it cape-style, fastening just the top button. Better for reading on the bus. With her doubts put to rest, she steps lively. From her parents' lower flat on Dexter, she's off to catch the eastbound on Grand River.

With spiritual confidence, young Marge knows that her relationship with God doesn't hinge on a particular brand of religion. The way she sees it, *He* doesn't care that she is choosing Wrigley's over Juicy Fruit. As long as she gives Him his due that He is eternal, all good, all knowing, all present, and almighty, and that He is her savior, she assures herself, she'll be fine.

Her decision to switch brands of religion to appease Tony's family is a political accommodation, pure and simple. God knows. She has no choice but to choose the path of least resistance to receive *his family's* blessing since there is no way they would ever accept a dark-hearted Protestant into their midst. So that's the course she takes, despite the angst it causes her own father, as she prepares to meet Tony's mother and father and four sisters.

Much like his Warsaw-born parents, two of his sisters are sweet and supportive. The other two leave her feeling cold and bewildered.

Despite a language barrier since they do not speak English, Marge connects with Tony's mom and dad without missing a beat. Speaking in Polish, they communicate with warm smiles, attentive nods and lots of hugs, all of which Marge understands. She enjoys their time together more than she could have imagined, as much for their steady eye contact as for the way they each hold one of her hands while they sit together on the sofa.

The two grumpy sisters are quite a different matter, however. Protective of their baby brother, they present a front Marge cannot begin to understand. Impossible to please, they have an ease at complaint over the smallest matters that serves to magnify their stone-faced indifference to their brother's bride-to-be.

On the drive from Detroit to meet his folks in the town of Jackson, seventy miles to the west, Tony is all sweet-talk. The cajoling stops the minute he turns into his parents' driveway. That's when he gives Marge an abrupt heads-up about what to expect with regard to his siblings. Granting that life is too short, Marge tells him that she has nothing to prove. As far as she is concerned, this visit is not about her. It is about the two of them and their future. That said, at Tony's request, Marge agrees to keep her smart style and confident ways under wraps that afternoon.

"Perfect, honey, that's perfect. Just don't slip off the couch while you're visiting."

Marge hasn't a clue what he is talking about as he grabs the door handle to let them in. When she figures it out at the end of the day, she breaks into a broad smile. They exchange a knowing glance when Marge realizes that she has been sitting on a two-year-old sofa that is still covered in factory-plastic. Her silk dress might have caused her to slide onto the floor had Tony not made that innocuous comment. *Very funny, chef. Very funny.* She grins.

Though far from her own style, on this day she views that plastic slipcover as a harmless cultural anomaly, much the way she views her future mother-in-law's delicate white lace doilies that are placed on every flat surface in her home. Most are on armrests or on side tables under candy dishes. Marge remembers a time when she might have been judgmental about such things. Not on this day, however. Today, she is in the company of her better angel; the one that rests on her shoulder as she sits with Tony's mom and dad, who smile often and pull her close and give her hugs. Truth be told, assuming the role of a demure fiancée makes for an enchanting afternoon for Marge.

It's dark when they say their good-byes. Tony kisses her hand as she slides to the middle of the bench seat of his three-year-old '42 Dodge. "You nailed it, baby doll. You nailed it."

He stays below the speed limit the entire way home. There is too much to soak in. He doesn't want their time together to end. Besides, Ann Arbor Trail is a blissful stretch at thirty miles an hour when your fiancée is at your side.

At last, they can allow themselves to talk about their wedding, which will occur a few Saturdays hence. Since Tony passed muster with Marge's mom and dad days before, everything is a go. Marge has but one more promise to keep before her wedding day.

Her religious instruction has been arranged through a few degrees of separation, thanks to a friend who knew a guy who sort of knew a priest over at St. Aloysius on Washington Boulevard, not far from Grand Circus Park. By city bus, it's a straight shot from her parents' home, where Marge keeps her Baltimore Catechism under wraps by necessity. She hides it in her room under her pillow so she can study at night after finishing her shifts. Lest she be thrown out of the house and onto the street, there will be no flaunting a book like that one, not in *her* father's home.

Her lessons begin.

Marge learns about *The Holy Trinity*. The priest directs her to acknowledge its mystery aloud, every time she makes the sign of the cross. Always punctual, she never misses a session, grateful that he has taken her on as a special favor. Aware of her timetable, the priest commits to make sure that she will finish her instruction before her big day.

Marge receives the Sacrament of Baptism on a Wednesday following a sparsely attended 9 o'clock morning Mass at cavernous St. Al's. Tony is busy with prep duty in the hotel kitchen. The ceremony takes place without fanfare before a handful of parish regulars, two of whom perform duties as witnesses by denouncing Satan, when asked. With oils and holy water at the ready, the priest's voice echoes throughout the near-empty church.

"*Margaret Mary, do you believe in God, the Father almighty, maker of heaven and earth?*"

"I do, Father."

"*Do you believe in Jesus Christ, his only Son, our Lord, who was born of the Virgin Mary, was crucified, died, and was buried, rose from the dead, and is now seated at the right hand of the Father?*"

"I do."

"*Do you believe in the Holy Ghost, the holy Catholic Church, the communion of saints, the forgiveness of sins, the resurrection of the body, and life everlasting?*"

"I do," she affirms.

"*This is our faith,*" the priest announces. "*This is the faith of the Church. We are proud to profess it, in Christ Jesus our Lord.*"

The entire congregation, such as it is, responds in unison. All four of them join with Marge to say, "*Amen.*"

The following Saturday brings one last "*I do.*"

It's her wedding day.

Marge's journey from spectator to active participant in the traditions of her new Church happens with no effort. She is enthralled with all the trappings, not the least of which is the ancient ritual of the Latin Mass with its mystical doctrine of transubstantiation. She also takes comfort knowing that there are seven Blessed Sacraments with special graces assigned to each. As long as she can remain steadfast and true, she will be provided with a pathway to Eternal Life.

She believes.

Having such a comingling of clarity and mystery at her disposal is nothing short of a miracle to Marge. With traditions dating back to St. Peter, the monolithic Vatican becomes a massive support structure for her. A source of daily spiritual sustenance, its Litany of Saints also supplies a spiritual benefactor for every occupation and situation. *Imagine. There is even a patron saint for "lost causes,"* she marvels, in praise of St. Jude. *Unbelievable. They've thought of everything.*

Fascinated by her new faith's rich history of heroes, Marge soon adopts one as her own.

St. Theresa of Lisieux, otherwise known as *"The Little Flower,"* becomes her guiding inspiration. Corresponding with missionaries on the far side of the world during the late 1800s, this young Carmelite was offered the opportunity to join a mission in French Indochina. As fate would have it, illness prevented St. Theresa from doing so. Her death from tuberculosis at the age of twenty-four would lead to a quick canonization.

From my earliest days, Marge raves about her youthful spiritual mentor; about how the example of St. Theresa gives her hope, and how that hope gives her confidence to dream. In fact, as Marge ponders the mystery of eternal reward, she reads about her spiritual mentor's version of Heaven, which would *"allow her to look after people on earth after she died."*

"God bless St. Theresa, Mikee. We share the same view, ya know, about what Heaven is, St. Theresa and me. Let's plant this rosebush in the backyard, why don't we? We'll do it in her honor. After all, she *is* up there looking after us down here. C'mon, buddy. Help me out, would ya? Let's put it on the fence line, next to the lilacs."

She hands me a spade. "Whatever ya need, Ma. I'll do whatever ya need," I tell her as I drop to my knees.

Marge talks as I dig. She tells me about the joy she takes from receiving *Absolution,* otherwise known as *The Sacrament of Reconciliation.* "That one Sacrament alone could turn the trick to get even *you* into Heaven, buddy."

Huh?

Of all the mysteries of her newfound faith, getting graces for going to confession is what Marge likes best about being a Catholic, she confides. "God knows, I need it."

Not one to mince words in a house filled with independent-minded progeny, she can't keep from cutting loose with expletives on Saturday afternoons. That's what makes her *Marge.* And whenever she does so, she always whispers in a way that makes me crack up. "Hey, Mikee, I'm not sure, but I may have said some bad words there."

I smile.

Ya think?

"Let's run up to Church and get a Mulligan, shall we? Come on, buddy." With that, we are out the door for a quick trip so she can say a proper *Act of Contrition* while I wait in a nearby pew.

Visiting the confessional becomes one of the simple joys of her life. Just as she takes pleasure in having a clean house every Friday, Marge loves starting over with a clean slate on Saturday afternoons almost as much as our dad enjoys golfing and bowling on weekends.

Despite those frequent lapses of her own, Marge doesn't tolerate profanity from any of us, I am first to learn. Surprise, surprise. Too young and too stupid to know better, I step in it big-time when I use a very bad word in her presence. Using me as an example for the entire family, she puts me in a headlock and shoves a bar of Ivory down my throat. Talk about disgusting. She would later tell me that mouth washings were a tried and true tradition when she was a young girl. I learned too late that my grandfather had established a soap-in-the-mouth ritual with her when she was six, as well. "So, don't feel bad, Mikee."

It is no consolation.

It's a few weeks later. Marge is alone in the kitchen when I see her shoulders rise and touch her ears. A master at anticipation, wincing is not part of her repertoire. Nothing ever surprises Marge, at least not in my presence. Until now, as I watch her face contort like she has just taken a gulp of sour milk straight from the carton.

Nino is unaware that she overheard him tell me, out of the blue, that Santa Claus doesn't exist. *What a dipshit.* It's the middle of summer, for Christ's sake. I want nothing more than to rage on him. But since Marge is within striking distance, I think better of it. Instead, I respond by scuffing the floor with my foot and saying the word "*shoot,*" which I am sure is a harmless utterance.

Nino is true to form when he runs off to tell her to grab the soap. "Mikee said a swear word *again,* Mom," he tattles.

Huh? Is "shoot" a swear word? Holy crap. At this point, I am way too deep in the *MikeeZone* to know what's what.

Nino whines again, "Mikee said *shoot,* Mom. Plain as day. I heard him. He said *shoot.*"

Marge replies in heroic fashion when she lets her nine-year-old have it. "Hey! Nino." His head snaps. "Cut the crap. I do not have time for your flippin' nonsense. Do not make things up. Be nice to your brother. And stop being a tattletale. I'm over it. Now, get outta my sight. Pronto. Beat it."

It was something beautiful to watch him scamper away.

Marge finds me a minute later. Laying her hands on my shoulders, she looks me in the eye. "Listen up here, buddy. Santa is as real as real can be, Mikee. He's as real as your dreams, believe you me. Oh, and thanks for not hitting your brother. I know you wanted to haul off and smack him good. That's all he wanted too, you know. He wanted you to hit him so he could throw a little fit and get you in trouble with me. You're a smart boy. Santa is not going to forget that when next Christmas comes along. Believe me. Just don't lose hope, Mikee. There's nothing worse. Take it from me, little one. Been there, done that. It's been four years since the dark days, back when your dad and I were drowning in booze. We came within a whisker of losing all hope."

Three days sober, Marge is home from the hospital with Patrick. Holding her newborn in her arms, she broaches the subject of a change of environment with Tony. She tells him that they have outgrown the duplex they're renting on Prevost, a few blocks from Our Lady Gate of Heaven, where their pride and joy, their daughter is in third grade.

"We're a family of six now, dear."

Tony is doe-eyed. He's looking at her like he had never quite learned how to count past five. "Huh?"

Tony. Tony. Tony.

Marge presses. "Don't you think it's high time we bought a house of our own, darling?"

It doesn't take long for Tony to realize that this might be the opportunity he's been waiting for to please the love of his life like never before. He scrapes together a down payment for a two-story, three-bedroom brick colonial a mile west. A unique style of home in an area where nondescript, 900-square foot bungalows dominate, it is still well within Detroit's western border in a neighborhood that has become an enclave for municipal employees, firefighters and policemen who are required to live within city limits. To Marge, it feels suburban.

Homeownership means a new school for Kathy. For Marge and Tony, it means acclimating to a new parish where young families dominate. Bound by common interests and common needs, it is a close-knit, supportive community, ideal for raising broods of Catholic kids.

Until then, they had been members of a somewhat older congregation, which allowed them to worship in relative anonymity. Now they realize that life in the community of Saint Suzanne will be different. With the bulk of parents in their same age group, everyone knows everyone else's business. And even when they don't, they act like they do.

Before boxes can be unpacked, a welcome party is organized.

Marge and Tony are pleased to find themselves at the center of attention among new neighbors with names like Bunny and Wil, Eileen and Tommy, Mary, Elmer, George and Libby. As families assemble in front of a garage in the backyard of a home in the middle of the block, Marge turns on her Irish charm, warming the dozen mothers who have gathered. Tony spins his own unique brand of self-effacing goodwill with the men huddled on the driveway.

They are a hit. They love their new neighbors. Tony and Marge could not be happier. German legend notwithstanding, Faust is a dream come true.

So far, so good.

Casseroles cover an eight-foot aluminum folding-table. A bouquet of delectable aromas fills the yard. In potluck fashion, Italian, Polish and German cuisines complement traditional American fare, like macaroni salad and corn on the cob. The bar is inside the garage. It consists of two galvanized steel laundry tubs, filled to the brim with loose ice and cold *Stroh's*. An adjacent card table is the hard liquor station, which sits next to a third tub loaded with bagged ice. Canadian whiskey, vodka, gin and an assortment of mixers like *Canada Dry Tonic*, *Vernor's* and *Squirt* fill a table. For the kids, every color of *Faygo* in the rainbow is on ice. By neighborhood standards, it is an extravagant bash.

Not wishing to appear ungrateful, Marge puts an end to well-intentioned overtures to *"relax and enjoy a cocktail."*

"You are all very kind, and it's so nice getting to know you. But there's something you should know."

The gathering grows quiet.

"Since the birth of our baby a month ago, Tony and I have *quit* drinking," she announces. "In fact, we joined AA," she tells them.

"Isn't that great," says one flat, anonymous voice from among the many.

The rumor mill would soon shift into overdrive.

As Marge tells it, normal gossip has to do with such things as workplace promotions, layoffs, teen pregnancies, or trips to juvenile court. Now, with two card-carrying AA members living among them, their new neighbors don't quite know what to think. It's a time when most people believe alcoholics sleep in cardboard boxes, if they aren't already in jail.

An informal welcome committee from the Catholic Church soon arrives on our front porch. Three women stand and fidget.

"Alcoholics? In our parish? We'll just have to see about that," they agree.

They have no idea what to make of this surefooted, spirited mother of four who has yet to miss Mass on Sunday. All they know is what they have heard about Marge and Tony, whose circumstances are an absolute disgrace.

Knock, knock.

They are greeted by Marge's trademark smile.

Under the guise of representing an obscure service organization, the ladies make themselves at home. Marge offers coffee. When she returns to the living room, an inquisition begins. "Remind us, if you would, dear. Where did you go to school and to which parish did you belong growing up?" they inquire.

Marge explains that she converted to Catholicism eight years before, a few days prior to her marriage. Polite and firm, she is proud to add that she attended public schools and that her parents are staunch Protestants.

"Oh, my." The ladies squirm. They can't believe they are sitting in the home of an avowed alcoholic and a convert to boot! God forbid. What is their beloved parish coming to?

Reading their reaction, Marge has half a mind to tell them that her children have been adopted like puppies off a street corner as well.

"For the life of me, Mikee, I could not figure out why they were so self-righteous. I gave them more than the time of day, didn't I? Oh, what am I saying? You weren't even two years old then. You would have had no idea. Nonetheless, I gotta tell ya, there was a period of time when the sour attitude of those ladies was breaking my spirit. I didn't want to leave the house. All I wanted to do was stay home and out of sight."

Deep sigh. She tries to smile.

The look on her face makes me sad.

A big sip of coffee seems to help. "So here's what I did, buddy. Do you want to hear it? I dealt with those attitudes the same way AA taught me to deal with the drink. I took a day at a time. I prayed for the serenity to accept the things I could not change, and I steered well clear of those gals. And guess what? As soon as I started praying for serenity, God blessed me with a remarkable boost of energy. All of a sudden, I was able to go about my business with a passion. Between my newfound sobriety and my faith, along with my beautiful family, I stopped worrying about what other people were thinking. I can't begin to tell you how good it felt just to let it go, Mikee."

Huh?

She still looks sad.

I hate seeing her like this.

"Come over here, my little sparrow. I need a hug."

She pulls me close and offers a smooch to the top of my head followed by a whisper in my ear. Her words make me smile. "Sometimes I wonder what we would do if we didn't have each other, buddy."

It's not long before the news of Nino's calling to the priesthood makes Marge into something of a neighborhood celebrity. That's when the judgmental attitudes of those ladies turned. Alcoholic, convert or whatever, as the mother of a boy who is going to become a priest, they now deemed Marge worthy to join their selective clique. They even invited her to sit with them in their first row pew at Mass one morning.

"Oh. That's very kind, but I already have my place. Thank you. I'm fine in the third row. But I'll see you there." Marge keeps her distance.

She had known for some time that those ladies never belonged to a community service organization, which is the one reason she let them into our house in the first place. A nosy bunch, they made it their primary business to keep track of who attended Mass most often and who prayed loudest in church. They were also known to make veiled comments about "*those types*" when referring to people of other races, religions or status, some of whom lived in a public housing project called *Herman Gardens*, a handful of blocks away.

"I pray for them, nevertheless, Mikee," she confides. "I just don't get how they can be so off-putting, with their high and mighty attitudes. They act like they're better than everyone else. It's as if they know a secret that they are not willing to share."

Meanwhile, the College of Cardinals is convening. A papal conclave is about to elect a new Bishop of Rome. Marge is about to adopt a new hero.

Her respect and affection for Pope John XXIII runs deep because of his efforts during the Holocaust to liberate refugees. Her "Good Pope John" would also become the first Pontiff in 400 years to meet with the Archbishop of Canterbury. By doing so, he would begin to deliver Marge's adopted, two-thousand-year-old Church into the modern era by convening the Second Vatican Council, in an effort to open her new Church to orthodox and Protestant alike. Finding herself on both sides of that religious divide, she viewed Pope John XXIII's ecumenism as a source of vindication. She adored him for that.

Just like her Pope with the big heart and the bulbous proboscis, Marge could never view her spirituality in *"us versus them"* terms. "God doesn't distinguish between kissing a prayer rug or celebrating the Miracle of Lights at Synagogue, Mikee. We are all His children. Got it?"

Uh-huh.

"Hey, buddy, here's another one for you. No one is perfect, and no one knows that better than God. How about that?"

Huh?

"Just as every person on this earth is capable of contributing to a better world, God also knows that we are all sinners. But at the end of the day, He still loves every one of us. How great is that? You know God loves you, right, Mikee?"

"Of course, Ma."

"That's all you need to know, buddy. As long as we confess our faults and ask for forgiveness, God always forgives. Got it?"

She beamed when she shared that one with her little sinner.

Riding the energy boost she gained from sobriety, Marge begins taking part in parish activities that involve a much less self-important group of women than those who visited a month before. Now a sacristan-member of the St. Suzanne *Rosary Altar Society*, Marge is part of a seasonal rotation that decorates the church, tidies the sacristy, and launders altar linens. Some in her new group make dressings for parishioners with untreatable malignancies. Absent fanfare, they gather every Wednesday to sew *Cancer pads*.

"Oh Mikee, I am so lucky to have found a group of gals whose hearts are in the right place. I just hope we're all earning graces for our deeds. I'm offering mine up. God knows I'll need them to get into Heaven."

Huh?

"I said that I need all the graces I can get, Mikee…you know, to compensate for my sinning ways. I'm flawed, buddy." Flashing a grin, she studies my reaction.

Sinning ways? My own mother?

Watching my jaw drop delights her to no end.

In the years that follow, Marge volunteers to teach Catechism on Monday afternoons to girls attending Cody. She says it keeps her feeling young. She also loves a soapbox. Good turnouts are guaranteed, since the girls are barred from attending parish-sponsored dances if they skip Catechism class. Known as *Teen Towners*, those Monday evening get-togethers in the basement of our Church are a perfect opportunity for public school girls to get groped by nice Catholic boys while dancing to songs like "*Angel Baby*." Yay God. Teaching Catechism class also gives Marge an opportunity to lend a non-judgmental ear to her students, many of whom have come to view her as something of a mentor. For most, she is the first person of authority in their young lives who listens to them.

As Marge is gathering paperwork one afternoon after class, a whisper from a sophomore beckons. "Got a minute?"

"Absolutely, Mary. What's up?" Marge sets her study planner aside.

"I think I'm pregnant, Mrs. F."

"Oh, dear. Talk to me, honey. How late are you? Have you seen a doctor?" Marge encourages her to sit.

"No, not yet, but I have a feeling the news won't be good." Tears stream.

"Tell me what happened, dear. Take a breath."

"I was in the backseat of Joey's car, Mrs. F. He put his hand under my sweater and then I felt his tongue in my mouth. I tried to be strong, but I couldn't stop. I kissed him back the same way, even though I knew I was being violated."

"Mary, what do you mean *being violated*? Be specific, honey."

"He *French-kissed* me, Mrs. F! We were in the backseat of his car! I'm sure I'm pregnant...."

After two more questions Marge realizes that there is no way on God's green acre that this sixteen-year-old could have gotten knocked-up, not if what she said was true. The poor thing had heard too many stories about what happens to innocents in the backseats of cars.

"Oh, Christ in Heaven, Mary, how old *are* you? We need to have a talk."

Marge would soon use that conversation as an opportunity to engage in a benchmark discussion with me about *"the birds and the bees."* Using that girl's confusion as the setup, she lays out *The Facts of Life* in such casual fashion that it doesn't faze me a bit. I am well on my way to school before it all hits me.

Holy Schmoly, Mom.

I could not believe that I just had a conversation like that with my very own mother.

Marge ended our little chat that day by dispelling a few rumors about a Westside institution called Vista Maria, where *unwed mothers* would go to avoid scrutiny while waiting out their pregnancies. Contrary to what I had heard, the nuns were not cloistered, they did not take vows of silence, and the girls did not have to spend every hour of every day making communion wafers as penance for sinful behavior. "Those sisters are doing God's work over there," Marge reminded me.

All of that was later confirmed by my neighbor Eddie, the paper plate artist whom I admired so. Despite having a reputation as a prince of raging hormones, he convinced those Sisters of the Good Shepherd over at Vista Maria to hire him to work there, since his mom had done so for years.

My hero.

All the while, when Marge isn't teaching Catechism or raising her young family, or cleaning the house, or attending school events, or laundering altar linens, or setting an example by attending Mass, she is dedicating her time to counseling others as an AA sponsor. Because she knows first-hand that addiction to alcohol doesn't discriminate by background or income, her sponsored souls comprise a diverse network, some of whom are distinguished Detroiters.

Tony, of course, attends meetings as well.

Through their involvement in AA, it becomes clear that whatever they lack in formal education or standing, they more than make up for with social adeptness. Thanks to *"The Program,"* as Marge calls it, they make friends from all around the city. Alcoholism becomes a blessing in disguise, even though common perception is that if you need help, you are a deviant. That's a notion that Marge finds amusing whenever she recalls her defiant late night boozing, shoulder-to-shoulder with gangsters and politicians, when she and Tony were working at the hotel bar. At this stage, she doesn't *"give a shite"* what others think about their addiction.

So she devotes herself to the program with everything she has.

Marge is chatting with her Northwest Group chapter leader at the end of a Monday evening meeting. "Let me get this straight. Are you telling me that you can't find anyone to go on TV to talk about *the program* in a closed meeting format? I can do that. Just tell me where and when," Marge offers.

You go, girl.

And so it is. Within a year of moving to Faust and kick-starting the neighborhood rumor mill by announcing their involvement in AA, Marge begins making Sunday afternoon television appearances on behalf of the program. Following Sunday Mass, a fellow Northwest Group member drives her to the studio of Detroit's CBS affiliate. Marge does the rest. As soon as she settles in, they ask her to do a ten-second promotional spot. Without hesitation, she hits her mark and looks deep into the camera lens, with a gaze that would make Mr. Rod 'Twilight Zone' Serling proud. Eyes sparkling, she approaches it like she is talking to an old friend. *"Hello, my name is Marge F. and I'm an alcoholic. Please join us, Sunday at noon, for a candid discussion."*

That's a wrap.

It doesn't take long for concerns about privacy to catch up with the show. The producers respond by instituting a policy of *"lone ranger-style masks"* to protect the identity of everyone on set. As a panelist, Marge talks about how the program changed her life and saved her marriage, while never once casting aspersions.

Meanwhile, with his cooking career flourishing, Tony keeps his promises. He stays sober, and stays out of Marge's way so she can care for the kids. He never raises a hand to his children. He also brings home his paycheck each and every week so the love of his life can run a proper household, all of which pleases Marge. Needless to say, when Marge is happy, Tony is happy.

There is just one little problem.

ELEVEN

YES, CHEF

Turning over his paychecks is getting old fast. Since joining AA, outside of work, Tony's recreational pursuits are all he has. And everything costs money. He needs a second income. Therein lies the rub. Given his life station and skill-sets, employers aren't lining up.

Then something happens.

Near the back door of the ad agency's kitchen on East Larned is Tony's walk-in. Twice a week, he signs off on morning deliveries. This day has him getting a jump on a veal stock for a savory Hungarian stew, which he'll season with fine rose paprika. A simple sweat of mirepoix and a splash of rich Burgundy will add depth of flavor. He'll be serving it on a bed of buttered egg noodles with a dollop of crème fraiche, and some sprinkles of flat-leaf parsley with a side of braised red cabbage. There will also be a fish entrée, with steamed vegetables, scratch-made *Parker House* rolls, three salad options and a cart full of extravagant desserts. If Tony knows anything, he knows how to delight a room full of advertising executives and their martini-sipping clients, all of whom he counts among his friends.

As he returns his clipboard to its peg, the produce driver confesses relief that the chef was on time to take a 7a.m. delivery. "We'll see you later then, Tony. I gotta get going. This is just the first of twenty stops I am making today. I've got bars and restaurants all over town."

Cue the light bulb.

Out the door by 6:15 each morning, Tony is long gone by the time we get up for school. Monday to Friday, business lunches are his primary responsibility. It allows him to knock-off by 3:30 most days. A few times a month, he works late to prepare elaborate dinners for corporate accounts from firms like General Electric, Gillette Safety Razor, Pittsburgh Plate Glass and Heinz "57," who fly into town to be wined and dined in the Maxon, Inc. executive dining room.

When he is not working late, his schedule allows him plenty of time to golf with his buddy Chet, the PGA Pro for Detroit's six *munis*. In spring and fall, that's where he finds his nirvana, *"chasing whitie,"* as he calls it, on public courses with names like Rackham, Rouge and Chandler Park. In summer, he cooks for the executive team at a business retreat owned by the ad agency up north on Black Lake, where it's rumored that Lucille Ball and Desi Arnaz spent their honeymoon back in the forties, guests of Mr. Lou Maxon himself. In winter, Tony is a fixture at Crown Lanes, our neighborhood bowling alley, where he captains a team in the St. Suzanne Men's Club League every Friday night at nine. On Sundays, he pleases Marge by dressing in a suit coat and tie to assume the duties of an usher at our church, which makes us all proud.

After Mass, he heads down into the shadows of the John F. Ivory Moving and Storage Co. to a small, nondescript bowling establishment called Argyle Lanes. That's where he meets up with a band of associates who never show themselves in our immediate neighborhood, perhaps because the police commissioner lives down the block. Perhaps not. Tony and Marge both came to know them during their days at the Belcrest. After-hours regulars, they were the same gentlemen who convinced them to call their first-born son and namesake *Nino*, which means *"Little Anthony"* in Italian. Known to a select few around town as *soldato*, they work in the shadows as foot soldiers in a far-reaching family business.

From the moment they tell Tony that they will consider taking him on as *an associate*, his spirits lift. It will allow him to capitalize on his God-given charm that makes everyone he meets feel like one of his best friends.

A new chapter unfolds when everyone's best bud, Tony, begins to moonlight as a bookie in a town with no mercy for slackers slow to pay—or for bookmakers slow to collect. With Tony up before dawn and home late, his soul mate Patrick is the only one except for Marge who knows about his dad's little side business. It is not even on the radar for Kathy, and of course not for Nino and me, no doubt as a concession to Marge.

It does not take long for Tony to become familiar with protocol. Slow-pays must be disciplined, sometimes in public. With reputations on the line, patience is not an option; not if you work for the crew with whom Tony has thrown-in.

They tell him it's all about volume, and if he can generate a sufficient amount of business, they will have his back regarding *client relations*.

"Make your nut and you'll have nothing to worry about, Tony. We'll take care of any unpleasantries," they pledge.

With that, Tony becomes connected.

He starts by recruiting his food suppliers. Like busy honeybees, they agree to pollinate their delivery routes on his behalf. His network grows. With him being happy to acknowledge their value, the more his food suppliers seed clouds, the more he spiffs his rainmakers. Before long, the best meat, fish and produce purveyors in the city are running numbers and stipulated odds for sporting events to bars and restaurants all over town. Even his equipment suppliers get in on the action.

As the beneficiary of occasional displays of public strong-arming, Tony earns a certain prestige around town. Already confident about walking into a room full of strangers despite his modest physical stature, his newfound status makes his swagger more pronounced.

Meanwhile, Tony's youngest begins shadowing his father as his dad's personal little *wise guy*. Blessed with an old soul and a quick wit, Patrick would do anything to spend more time with his dad. Were Tony an organ grinder, he would have been honored to don a colorful little suit and dance on a string to help his father better engage his audience.

Marge transitions by looking the other way. Despite the reality that Tony is exposing their youngest to a culture of gambling and God knows what else, she convinces herself that her husband and her baby are just bonding, as they have been doing since Patrick was in a high chair. Besides, Tony *has* stayed true to his word. He *is* still sober and he *is* still turning over his paychecks from the ad agency, after all. Marge can't complain. Her hands are full anyway.

Patrick transitions as well. The adorable mascot becomes a skilled accomplice when Tony starts spiffing him, too. Pleased to have a few bucks in his pocket each week, Tony's second-grader begins accompanying his father to his Friday night bowling outings, which let out sometime around midnight. Post-league wagering continues across the street, among restaurant patrons at *The Americana* on Plymouth, where Tony takes action from all comers on the number of "silver dollars" his little boy can consume. Hungry by habit, Patrick never lets him down. Tony always wins, thanks to a son who loves consuming little pancakes almost as much as he loves pleasing his dad.

Through it all, those Friday night shenanigans remain hush-hush. Big secret.

What is no secret is that Tony is a recipe guy. The spontaneity needed in raising a family is beyond him. Time and again, he proves it.

Despite his hectic schedule, Tony makes a point of coming home every Thursday night for his *Untouchables* fix. It's during those evenings, at home with his kids watching Robert Stack as straight-shooting Eliot Ness, when our dad exhibits a knack for speaking without thinking, for which he is always in need of redemption. Mocking Nino's preference for schoolwork over sports, he wisecracks by calling his namesake "a little fairy" in front of everyone. It lands him squarely in Marge's *chateaux bow-wow*.

Knowing that it's not an isolated episode of disparagement, Marge speaks her mind. "If you're gonna be home, I need you to act like an adult, damn it," she scolds, before letting him have it. "I don't give a flat-ass hump how you do it, just fix it, Tony."

Whoa.

In an attempt to get back into her good graces, our dad agrees to make a rare appearance on a Wednesday night to take charge of his oldest boy's tenth birthday celebration. Marge lays down the ground rules. It's time to show Nino and all of his friends from the neighborhood how much we love him.

"I will take care of the invitations, the decorations and dessert," she explains. "You'll be in charge of the birthday menu, cooking and serving—and don't forget; we're talking about a roomful of ten-year-old kids here, Tony." Marge says it like he needs a reminder.

An enormous round table sits in the middle of our unfinished basement. A twelve-top by ballroom standards, it is surrounded by twenty small metal folding chairs. Birthday balloons and crepe paper hang from the exposed pipes above. As children assemble, Tony enters with dramatic flair. He's clicking a pair of silver tongs, dressed in his finest *kitchen whites*. Too bad for us. Without his tall hat, he looks less like a chef than a mad man from some Frankenstein movie.

That cannot be his intent. *Can it?*

Expecting hamburgers or hot dogs, the kids giggle when Tony puts a lemon wedge on each plate. Confusion sets in as he begins placing ramekins of drawn butter around the table. Then, a hotel pan and a steaming platter appear. Birthday decorations wilt. Like a science project gone awry, balloons bob as steam rises from his tray that overflows with hot cobs of corn and boiled blood red crustaceans. There must be a dozen lobsters on that platter surrounded by two dozen steaming ears. Talk about overcompensating. Even for Tony, it's a stretch.

Horrified children coil next to the laundry tub that's filled with ice and soft drinks. Some cower beneath the table. Others sit in shock and scream.

Even I could tell it wasn't going well.

The last time these kids from Faust saw a lobster would have been at the library in a dusty reference book.

Marge saves the day when she calls everyone to attention. "Ok, kids…if you prefer, just eat some corn and then you can enjoy birthday cake and ice cream."

Disaster averted.

With that the party is a success. As the singing concludes, Nino blows out the candles and opens his big present. A chemistry set! Marge knew what he wanted. Everyone cheers.

In the midst of the commotion, I see her glance at Tony. She rolls her eyes, and then gives him a smile. Feeling my gaze, she tosses her favorite seven-year-old a wink as if to say, "*At least your dad tried.*"

Truly. He did.

Tony continues to stay out of the doghouse by making sure we eat well. Commercial food suppliers make regular visits to our home. From downtown, they find their way to the corner of Faust and West Chicago, hang a left, and then back-in to the second driveway past the medical clinic to unload delicacies at our door. So regular are those visits, Marge greets each driver by name, always with a smile. The deliverymen respond in kind.

Punctuated by oohs and aahs, inspections of each package follows. Marge loves it when there is enough food to share with the priests at church and sometimes with grateful neighbors. As for making her proud, those deliveries work like a charm, every time.

Oblivious to our dad's secret side-career, Kathy, Nino and I assume that those deliveries are just perks for having a father who is a popular chef in a big city.

Live Maine lobster, anyone?

Every Thanksgiving JL Hudson sponsors a parade on Woodward, although we never go. Lions Football is the lone event worthy of Tony's attention on Thanksgiving when the Packers are in town. At Marge's insistence, he always gets four tickets in case Nino wants to join, but he never does. So, "Tony the Chef," as he is known, looks proud as he waves to his friends while directing Patrick and me up and down the aisles of Tiger Stadium, through the sell-out crowd, to our section on the fifty yard-line. Ever the high roller when the weather cooperates, he directs us to use Nino's seat for our coats, providing he hasn't already scalped the ticket.

His annual nod to parenting occurs at the start of that game when he reminds us that hot dogs will not be available after the half, since Marge and Kathy are at home preparing our big feast. On that one day each year we can count on our dad to make an appearance at our dinner table.

Marge cooks. Tony carves. Patrick sets off a chain reaction by making me laugh when I take my first sip of milk. As white liquid shoots out my nose, Nino and Kathy cringe in disgust. Tony applauds Patrick's timing. I earn a healthy swat from Marge for making a god-awful mess.

More than turkey with all the trimmings, earning a swift swat at our dining room table becomes my own personal Thanksgiving tradition.

And so my whackings began.

TWELVE

THE FRANCHISE

Taking full ownership of her discipline franchise, I become a target rich environment for Marge when she begins using me as her exclusive example of punishment for disobedience. Whack! Whack! Whack! I'm incapable of avoiding her swift open hand. She is one quick mother.

"Better get used to it, Mikee. Just remember what your grandfather used to say to me when I was your age, and look how I turned out. *"Margaret, I wouldn't hit you if I didn't fookin' love you."*

God help me.

Since Kathy internalizes her values, she never needs discipline. Nino's fragile demeanor and pending-priest status makes him off limits as her ticket to Heaven. Patrick is too young for corporal punishment. Besides, by this time, he has fallen under our sober dad's wing. That leaves Marge's faithful confidante hanging out by my lonesome. Clueless. I'm the frog in tepid water oblivious that the pot might be about to boil.

The space race is on. Squished into the nose of a Jupiter ballistic missile, space monkeys Able and Baker and their recent exploits have put us back in the game.

USA! USA! USA!

It's a magnificent rain-soaked Sunday. Right after Mass, I head out to the middle of Cody with my next-door neighbor Lee to turn a rusty six-yard cement mixer into a space capsule of our very own. After figuring out how to operate the release aperture to flip, turn and spin the vessel, it's countdown time. I crawl in first. Six inches of wet concrete goop at the bottom of that bucket doesn't slow me down one bit. Turn. Spin. Turn. Spin. We carry on for hours.

Heading home, I am blissfully unaware of the mud covering every inch of my body. It's not until I walk through the door that I realize I have been mummified.

Crap. I'm doomed.

Earlier that morning, Marge had made an announcement. We would all be going to a big event at our Parish Hall that evening. It's time for *The Tenth Annual St. Suzanne Spaghetti Dinner*. Our dad will be cooking for the entire parish, which is a first. Marge is proud and excited. Hundreds of families will be in attendance, she tells us, so it is essential that we wear our Sunday best and be ready, on time, to support our dad.

"Got it, Mom!" I tell her.

Pushing through the side door, I find her in the kitchen. She's wearing a light-wool mid-calf skirt, stockings, and black high-heels. She has a soft gray sweater thrown over the shoulders of her long-sleeved silk blouse. She is a vision of tasteful gray on gray on gray. She looks terrific.

"Hey, mom!"

She smiles.

Phew. All is well. Thank you, God.

Oops. Patrick, Nino and Kathy are already sitting in the living room, dressed and ready to go. As the concrete continues to cure, I am realizing that Marge does not feel as good as she looks. Squinting at my muddy stiff state, her jaw drops before she can say the words that I most dread.

"Mikee, get over here right now and I won't hit you."

Shoot.

From around the corner comes Patrick's whisper. "Pssst! Run, muh-Mikee, run!"

We both know what's coming.

Knowing better, I dismiss all thoughts of scrambling, since it would make matters worse. Our dad is already at his station in the kitchen of the church basement, for God's sake. Every minute is precious. Hoping for the best, I move in close. After all, she did say she wouldn't hit me.

Dipping her shoulder, she gives the back of my head a mighty cuff with her open right hand.

Thwaaack!

Whoa. I pitch forward.

"You should have come sooner, Mikee."

I'm beginning to see stars when Patrick's commentary begins in earnest. "Ooooh. That was a big one, la-la-ladies and juh-juh-gentlemen...muh-Mikee could be down for the ca-count here...."

He watches her drag me up the stairs.

On the landing, she boxes my right ear, this time with an open-handed roundhouse left. She's unbelievable. I'm flying through the air now, clothes and all, as she tosses me from the hallway into the bathtub.

"Look at you! What the hell were you thinking, Mikee?"

Off come my clothes.

"Did I say hell? I asked you a question, young man. Did you make me commit a sin? Did you make me say hell?"

Patrick bears witness. "Yup, yup. That is wa-wa-what you said, Ma. You said *hell.* Mmmm-Mikee muh-made you."

Thwaaack!

After blessing herself for using profanity, I earn a final cuff as she proceeds to massage the concrete out of my hair. She even scrubs between my toes.

By the end of that humiliating experience, I am desperate to figure out a way to put this whacking business behind me once and for all.

Please, Lord, make it so.

THIRTEEN

THE AGE OF ANXIETY

I don't get it. Marge's smack-a-thons have become ridiculous. All I can do is pray that we'll put all of this behind us next week when the two biggest events of my young life come to pass. First Confession and First Holy Communion are approaching. At long last, I will reach the *Age of Reason*.

I pray that will change everything.

Marge insists we ride the bus downtown to prepare for my big week ahead. We're off to St. Aloysius to pay a visit, light a candle, and do a bit of shopping at the Archdiocese Bookstore next door. That's where Catholics can buy crucifixes with sliding compartments that contain little candles and scented oils, just in case a priest has to be called to perform *Last Rites* at the house. Ugh. It's the saddest of the Seven Blessed Sacraments by far, that one. From what I've heard, barring a miracle, as soon as they pull out the old Extreme Unction oils, you die.

Marge is excited for me. She can't stop talking as we wind our way downtown. She tells me that we will be buying a small white *missalette* that I will use during First Communion. After Mass, she says, she'll place it in a shoebox for posterity alongside Kathy's bronzed baby shoes. She also tells me a *two-fer* is in the offing. She's planning on buying me a scapular, as well, to commemorate my First Confession.

This sounds big.

Steeped in mystery, scapulars are cloth medallions that are worn around the neck like a dog tag after children reach *The Age of Reason*. Marge views it as an insurance policy that just might guarantee my avoiding the fires of Hell.

When she puts it that way, I'm all for it.

Although common teaching is that God cannot be manipulated, legend has it that if you die with a scapular on, it gives you a leg-up in getting into Heaven. It goes without saying that any kid who ever heard that one made darn sure that their scapular was blessed. They also made sure never to take it off, even in the shower. Spotting those cloth medallions became the easiest way to identify Catholic kids from surrounding parishes in the Cody pool on open swim nights.

"Only with a proper blessing can a scapular become *invested*," Marge continues; whatever the heck that means. "So you'll need to be sure to get it blessed right after your First Confession. Got it, Mikee?"

"Got it, Ma. I got it," I promise.

In keeping with custom, she also confirms that as soon as it's blessed, I should never take it off. God forbid I should be flattened by a bus on my way to a ballgame.

"Thanks, Mom."

She is smiling as I stare out the window at a parade of taillights, challenging myself to name the make, model and year of each and every car we pass.

It helps me forget every word I heard.

"*Bless me Father for I have sinned….*"

After a proper Act of Contrition, I do what the priest inside the box behind the little screen tells me. Doing my penance doesn't take long.

One *Glory Be* later, I am off.

I can't begin to count the number of Saturdays when I tagged along with Marge to sit in a pew outside the confessional while she took her "Mulligans." This time, it's me that's heading home on a cloud of divine grace. I'm singing like a cherub as I march down West Chicago.

"Holy-Holy-Holy-Lord-God-Almighty…."

I'm pure!

Arriving in the kitchen, I see my little white blazer and white tie are hanging from the refrigerator door. Everything is ready for my big First Communion Saturday tomorrow. Marge greets me with a hug. "Let's have a look at that newly blessed scapular of yours, young man."

Uh-oh.

I forgot. It's still in the cubby of my desk.

I never even got it blessed.

"Get over here right now, Mikee, and I won't hit you."

Not again.

Out the door, I'm running for my life. Marge is motoring like an Olympian. She catches me behind the garage by my collar and cuffs me good. "I have half a mind to march you back to church, young man," she hollers, as she whacks my bottom as an encore admonishment for my cement mixer misadventure two weeks before. *Come on, Ma. Get over it, wudja?*

She is still trying to clean dried concrete from the tile surrounding our tub basin.

Grout schmout. Can't she see I am drowning in details here? *Hellooo.* Do I need to remind her that I am just a darn second grader? How am I supposed to remember all these rules and requirements? I can't even remember my mittens on cold afternoons.

God. I need a plan. Bad.

Desperate, I promise myself to keep Marge off the warpath by committing to become the best student I can be. That should do it. I am also holding out hope that a few good grades might result in the major reward that I have been dreaming about for as long as I can remember. Wag, wag. Lick, lick.

FOURTEEN

THE PENCIL SHARPENER

Third grade. My *Whack Avoidance Strategy* is falling into place when the toughest nun in school selects *me* to be part of an Advanced Reading Group.

This is huge.

I can't wait to get home to share the news with Marge. She hasn't had to chase me around the garage in months. And now that I am the lone boy selected to be part of this elite assemblage, I'm betting it just might result in that major reward.

Something good is about to happen. I can feel it.

Lord, don't take me now.

As the group gathers, I head to the back of the room to sharpen my pencil. An angel of a girl stands to do the same. As I fumble to push my blunt into the little hole, I find myself on the receiving end of the most gentle, sweetest kiss imaginable, right on my ever-loving lips. Then she holds it…*Holy crap*…for what feels like a lifetime.

I tingle all over.

Oh, dear Lord Jesus, whatever I did to deserve this, thank you.

God is great.

Shuffling to my seat, I gaze out the window. Sunbeams are streaming through puffy cumulous clouds.

It's an Ave Maria sky!

Birdies are chirping.

Life does not get any better than this. That's for sure.

"Step up here, mister."

Huh?

I glance toward the rostrum. Red-faced, the nun has one eye popping from below her starched white mantle. She's slapping a long wooden pointer into her hand. I haven't a clue who she's talking to until I feel her fingers pinch my ear.

She is yanking *me* to her desk? This is unbelievable. My classmates look on in horror. *Not the dreaded ear-pull. Not Mikee*, I can hear them thinking.

This has gotta be a mistake.

What the hell?

She is writing a note. She's sealing an envelope and pinning it to my shirt! *Did I mispronounce a word? Did I pick my nose? Was I slouching in my chair?*

"Excuse me, Sister. Could you please tell me what this is all about?"

Ouch!

The penguin-clad creature revisits the ear grab. "You know what you were doing, young man."

"Huh?"

"You were *playing* with yourself, mister," she screams for everyone to hear.

Holy shoot!

Talk about a buzz-kill. All around the room, mouths fall open wide. Eyes grow big as saucers. This cannot be happening. She cannot be serious. It has to be a mistake. Can you imagine the humiliation I would have endured had I sat in front of that room fiddling with my little sausage? She must think I'm insane. I *must* have misheard her. Taking a page from the book of Tony, I turn on the ol' Mikee charm.

"Excuse me, Sister. Could you repeat that for me, please? I'm afraid I didn't get your take there."

"I *said* you were playing with yourself, young man!" she bellows, even louder than before.

"No way, Sister. You've got the wrong guy!"

God help me.

From my very first day of school, Marge made one thing clear. *"Grades are irrelevant. Just don't screw up in conduct. Got it, Mikee?"* For Marge, conduct is all that matters, since that reflects on her and on our family.

I am in so much trouble.

"Settle down, mister. It's official. Your school day is over. Get home with this note to your mother straightaway."

Oh my God.

Given Marge's reaction to the cement mixer incident last year, I have a vague notion how she will respond to this. It is not going to be pretty. Whatever she ends up doing, I know one thing for sure. Our relationship will change forever.

This could be the big one.

Dear Lord in Heaven, please don't let her kill me.

Heavy feet make for a long walk home. I pause for prayer on West Chicago. *"Thirty days has September, April, June and November, all the rest....*

Unbelievable.

I've forgotten how to pray!

C'mon, Mikee. Think, boy, think.

I need oxygen.

Calling on the most formal appeal in my repertoire, I hope to God a little Latin will do the trick. To high Heaven I pray in the language I learned to become an altar boy. *"Suscipiat Dominus sacrificium de manibus tuis, ad laudem et gloriam nominis Sui, ad utilitatem quoque nostram, totiusque ecclesiae suae sanctae."* Then I switch to English. *"May the Lord accept this sacrifice at Your hands, to the praise and glory of His name, for our good and the good of all His Holy Church."* Then back to Latin. Then English. Then Latin.

"Mea Culpa, Mea Culpa, Mea Maxima Culpa."

I am *so* screwed.

Think, Mikee.

Ok. What if I were to go down big? What if I were to pretend that it's all true? Boy gets kissed. Nun gets pissed. I'll keep it simple. I'll just march into the kitchen and come clean.

That's what I'll do.

I try to imagine my attempt to explain that note. *"Uh…yeah, Mom. I messed up a little in conduct. That old nun was spot-on, God bless her. She caught me making-out with a girl next to the pencil sharpener. Then I marched to the front of the classroom and started rubbing myself through my pants; you know, I was sort of whacking-off during Advanced Reading, in front of all of my classmates, in full view of the nun. No big deal, really,"* I'd have added.

Marge would not be amused.

She really *is* gonna kill me.

As I pull open our side door, I reach for my scapular. It's still dangling from my neck. Thank God. At least I've got that going for me. Marge is where I knew she'd be. She's sitting at the kitchen table, sipping her coffee, reading a book.

"How was your day, my handsome little sparrow?" she smiles.

Ready for an onslaught, I brace myself against the fridge.

"My day was ok, Mom," I lie.

"What's that?"

"It's a note from a nun."

"Well come on over here. Let's see what it says."

While she reads it, I scroll through the names of every Saint I can remember. I finish with a plea to the Almighty. *Oh my God I am heartily sorry for having offended thee....*

When I look up, Marge is crumpling the note into a small wad. She's tossing it into the wastebasket. "You're fine, Mikee."

"Huh?"

"You knew what that note said, didn't you? But you still brought it home. I'm impressed. You're becoming quite a young man, aren't you? You did the right thing, buddy. I know coming straight home wasn't easy. Listen. I love you now and I'll love you forever. I may get a little amped up from time to time, but nothing you can do will ever make me love you less."

Unbelievable.

I was right about one thing.

Our relationship changed forever.

From one offspring to the next, the intensity of Marge's focus on us shifts every three years, between the ages of nine and twelve, when she begins sharing learning tools so we can each figure out on our own how to succeed. Up to that point, she sticks to her simple mantra: "*Just don't screw up in conduct.*"

By fourth grade, personal accountability is in play. Self-sufficiency rules. Homework assignments, science fair projects and event schedules become personal responsibilities. Refrigerator magnets do not exist. Not in Marge's world. Test tomorrow? Mass serving duties? Got practice after school? Figure it out.

Protocol never waivers.

Try asking the meaning of a word.

"Bring the dictionary, Mikee. You know where it is. It's on the bookshelf, at the top of the stairs, outside your sister's bedroom."

Always smiling, Marge never relents. When I return, she makes me say the word aloud before reciting the definition and using it in a sentence. Considering how much she reads, I am mystified that she doesn't know the meaning of any words.

Now, I'm uck-fayed. Again. Six of my seven math problems have been marked with a big red "X."

I stuff the evidence down my pants before greeting her in the kitchen.

"I don't think arithmetic likes me, Mom. I can't even spell that word."

"Hey. Arithmetic is a wonderful subject, Mikee, and it's not a difficult word to spell." She shares an acronym about a rat eating ice cream.

"Ah, I get it now." I thank her as I turn to bolt.

"Hold on there, cowpoke, one more thing." She stops me in my tracks.

"You have always been a boy in a hurry, Mikee. That's why I make you sit with both cheeks on your chair during dinner. That's why I ask you to hold onto the refrigerator handle or the edge of the sink while we chat. I do that so you don't run all over the place when we're talking, right?"

"Right, Mom." I shrug.

"So do me a favor. When it comes to arithmetic, don't be in a hurry. And before you start leaping to conclusions about liking it or not, remember this. Do you think it was easy for Kathy and Nino to become "Math All Stars" at St. Suzanne? Well, I can assure you it wasn't, not before I told them the secret."

"Huh? There's a secret?"

"Hell yes, there's a secret, Mikee. Haven't I told you about it? Now this is a good one."

I love it when my mom tells me secrets.

"Here's the deal, buddy. To be good at arithmetic, you need to know three things. That's all. You're a smart boy, right?"

I nod. "So what are the three things, Mom? What's the secret?"

"I will tell you but you have to promise to follow this direction each and every time you need to solve a problem in addition, subtraction, multiplication or long division. You promise?"

"I promise, I promise. Tell me. Tell me the secret, Mom."

"Ok. Here you go." Long Pause. Either she's thinking or she's teasing. It's killing me.

"First is, print your numbers clear. Don't be in a hurry when you're printing your numbers, Mikee, especially the number seven. I don't care what the nuns teach you. The point is, get the right answer. I always had success crossing the middle of number seven, like it's a backward letter "F," that way you don't confuse it with a *one*. Got it?"

"Cool, Mom. Print my numbers clear."

"The second thing is to align your numbers with care. Do that. Practice using graph paper if you have to. Just don't be in a hurry when you're aligning your numbers, Mikee."

"Align my numbers with care. Got it."

"Last but not least, and this is important, always check your work twice. Every problem, every time; check it twice before turning it in. Do you understand?"

"I get it, I get it. Print clearly, align my numbers, and check my work twice. Is that all I have to do to be good at arithmetic?"

"That's it, buddy. You're a smart boy. Just don't be in a hurry."

FIFTEEN

AN IRISH TOAST

Marge loves nothing more than sitting in her spotless kitchen with the scent of Spic-n-Span and a hint of Pine-Sol wafting about the room every morning. A good book and some music on our living room stereo makes for a perfect start to her day. Most days, she awaits my arrival so she can fuss to make sure that I am presentable to the nuns. *Teeth brushed? Check. Crisp white shirt? Check. Tucked-in all around? Check. Tie straight? Check. Trousers hitched? Check...Check...Check.*

Vettings, I call them. They drive me up the wall.

In civilized fashion, Marge drinks her coffee from a cup, never a mug. While Tony finds his nirvana golfing and bowling, Marge finds her little piece of Heaven in her clean kitchen each morning, enjoying her coffee black. And whenever precious drips pool on her saucer, a ritual begins. She sets the cup aside on a napkin and brings her little plate to her lips. As she sips, she makes sure to keep eye contact with me, as if no one else in the world exists. Then, with a wink that always makes me feel like we are sharing a one-of-a-kind moment, she whispers, cooing in triumph, "*Oooh, I make a good cup of coffee.*"

She calls that our version of an Irish Toast.

As for school-day logistics, she tackles them like an architect preparing for a design presentation. Before each of us hit the kitchen, lunches are bagged. Shirts are laundered. Shoes are shined. A warm egg sandwich is wrapped in foil ready to travel. Morning Mass awaits. *Quickies,* we call them, since the priest blasts through the liturgy on weekdays, unlike on Sunday mornings.

Dominus vobiscum.
Tada-dada-dada-da.

Kathy and Nino are long gone.

With one full bath in the house, we execute a phased delivery system. It gives Marge a bit of one-on-one time with each of us, except for Patrick, who, she readily concedes, "*is simply not a morning person,*" so her "*AA Baby*" is always the last out of bed. After having worked with him patiently to help him conquer his stammer, Marge cuts him slack like no other. As the only one of her boys who does not become a Mass server, she takes care to boost his standing with the nuns by loading his schoolbag with neatly wrapped gifts for him to deliver around the holidays.

"What are we talking about here, Mom? What's inside the packages?" Patrick presses, fearing they might contain something creepy like little samples of bath oils.

"Oh, they're just handkerchiefs, honey. Don't forget to give them to the sisters."

"Right, Ma. No problem," he promises.

A long-time student of the art of spiffing thanks to tutelage from our dad, young Patrick can appreciate the opportunity to be the bearer of gifts for the nuns. "Hmmm, handkerchiefs. Good idea, Ma," he praises her as he heads out the door.

It's the last day of school before Christmas when the principal approaches him on the playground. Feeling her presence, he raises his hands high in the air, even though his back is turned. "I didn't do it!" he protests.

"Calm down, Patrick. Everything is fine," she soothes him. "I just want to make sure that you and your mother know how grateful we are for the lovely nylon stockings you gave us."

Patrick shows no hint of surprise. Holding her gaze with a polite smile, he acts like he was in on it. "Sha-sure, Ssssister. Merry Christmas."

It's no wonder his morning ritual is so very different from mine. Marge lets Pat run out the door each morning with his shirttail flapping.

God love him.

The soundtrack from *West Side Story* has Marge in high spirits. Feigning a tin ear, she is humming off-key to, "*I feel pretty.*"

"How about him? Isn't Leonard Bernstein fabulous? Have we watched one of his Young People's Concerts? Oh, Mikee, remind me, would you? We should do that."

"Huh?"

I hate to break it to her but watching one of those concerts hasn't quite made my to-do list.

She calls him "*my Maestro.*" She says he's a genius whose achievements epitomize the promise of our culture. "He is an *American Original,*" she tells me.

"Boy oh boy, if I could meet anyone, Mikee, other than the Pope of course, *my Maestro* would be at the top of the list. From what I've read, we have a few things in common. We're both big fans of W.H. Auden, you know."

She had me there.

"Hey. Did I tell you about his performance after the inaugural?" She's on a roll. To hear her talk, you'd have thought that she attended one of those elegant receptions herself.

"Imagine. Linus Pauling and Leonard Bernstein chatting with John Glenn and e.e. cummings. Can't you just see it, buddy!"

She recounts one story over and over. It's the night President and Mrs. Kennedy were hosting dozens of Nobel laureates at the White House. Raising his glass, JFK proclaims it *"The most extraordinary collection of talent, of human knowledge, that has ever been gathered together at the White House, with the possible exception of when Thomas Jefferson dined alone."* Whenever she tells it, she always ends the same way, careful to remind me that Thomas Jefferson wrote the words, *"All men are created equal."* She loves sharing that anecdote almost as much as she loves her Irish-Catholic-Leader-of-the-Free-World for his dream of *"A New Frontier,"* which inspires her so.

Heading down the stairs, I liken my feelings of dread about Marge's vettings to the way I feel when she pre-empts my groans on Wednesday nights by offering up the words, "IT'S STEAK," whenever I smell liver frying in a pan for dinner. After holding my nose during grace, I eat what I can, lest I be knocked off my chair without warning.

From the top of the landing, I can picture Marge licking her hand as she readies to put down my cowlick, which I don't get at all. For God's sake, it's the essence of my personality.

She doesn't quite see it that way.

Just last week she noted that the *Brylcreem* didn't seem to be working so well. That was the morning I almost barfed all over my fresh-laundered shirt when she hoiked a goober of slippery spittle into her palm. She had to rub her hands together to melt it down a bit before pasting it all over my head. *Nice, Ma. Real nice.* Honest to God. Following that display, I knew I had to figure a way to get out the door without being slobbered. Never again, I swore. Never again.

Talk about disgusting.

A stack of books balance on the chair beside her.

"So what ya readin', Mom?"

She smiles. "Oh, I'm glad you asked. It's called *Deliver Us from Evil*. I've told you about Dr. Tom Dooley, right? This book is about his experience in Southeast Asia where he helped train villagers to care for thousands of their own in makeshift medical clinics. He was the President's inspiration in creating the Peace Corps. Did you know that? Dr. Dooley is a true hero if ever there was one. And he died so young. It's sad. We lost a saint of a man there, Mikee. Oh, look at the time. You'd better get going."

Success!

One morning down.

An eternity of mornings with no slobber to go.

Energized that I can actually make her ignore my cowlick, I start showing interest in whatever she is reading. Marge much prefers spending that time talking about her books or current events, anyway. And whenever she does, it's like we are just two friends having a conversation. That's how I came to know everything about novels by Morris West in the years that followed. It wouldn't be long before I was hearing about a book called *The Ambassador,* which has something to do with the crisis of Western diplomacy in Vietnam, wherever that is.

Searching for a passage, she makes me cringe when she licks her finger.

"Come on, Mom. Aren't we over that? Not again."

"Settle down, buddy. It's only for traction." She giggles as she turns the page. "Oh, you're gonna love this. Listen up here." She gestures for me to sit while she reads.

"Why do you come to this place?"
"To seek enlightenment."
"Why have you not found it?"
"Because I seek it."
"How will you find it?"
"By not seeking."
"Where will you find it?"
"In no place."
"When will you find it?"
"At no time."

"How about that one, Mikee? Isn't it mystifying? What a marvelous culture!" She beams.

You call that marvelous? Downright creepy, is all I can figure. "What the heck is it supposed to mean, Mom? I don't get it."

"You're not alone there, buddy. Our military leaders don't seem to understand much about that culture either. That passage is what's called a '*mondo.*' It's a form of meditative dialogue. Bottom line is that you don't need to understand it. That's the beauty of it. That's why they call it a meditation."

Huh?

From what I gather, West's novels are mostly about our Church. One of Marge's favorites, "*The Devil's Advocate,*" describes an appointee of the Pope who is tasked to argue *against* nominees for Sainthood.

"Inside the Vatican, that person has a title. He is known as the 'Official Skeptic,'" she tells me.

"Cool." I mean it.

Together we imagine conclaves of scholars around a big table in Rome, debating the merits of miracles by the likes of Dr. Tom Dooley, whose official petition for Sainthood Marge is supporting, despite recent assertions of his same-sex orientation, about which she could give a shite. Marge's God knows better. "He loves us all, Mikee. He loves us all."

The stack of books beside her grows. *The Shoes of the Fisherman* would soon find its way to the kitchen table. It's been more than a year since she first made mention of something called *The Berlin Wall*. "Imagine a Pope from a communist country. God, wouldn't that be something? You know, I often dream that I'm standing in St. Peter's Square, buddy, as part of a throng. Oh, Mikee, imagine being able to spot the Pope, even from a distance. I would be happy to stand shoulder-to-shoulder with tens of thousands of others. The crowd would not make a bit of difference. Not to me. Just to be able to stand in the square and watch the Holy Father wave to thousands of faithful and be one among many, Mikee. Can you imagine what that would be like?" She says it with a hearty sigh. "Now *that* would be a dream come true. Hey, you'd better get a move on. You don't want to be late."

As hard as I try, it's almost impossible to imagine that my very own mom has dreams too. As I head for the door, she takes me into her confidence. "Here's the way I see it, buddy. As long as I can dream, everything is right in the world. I dream, therefore I am."

Huh?

With images of Maestro-composers, Official Skeptics and Popes swirling in my head, I shoot a parting salvo of my own.

"Hey, Mom. Who are your heroes?"

Darn it. I definitely should have saved that one for a rainy day. She could have talked for an hour.

"I assume you mean in addition to *My Maestro*, Mikee? My Twentieth Century heroes are President John Fitzgerald Kennedy; Dr. Martin Luther King, Jr.; Bobby Kennedy; and Pope John XXIII, in no particular order, thank you."

I can feel her joy as I push through the door.

SIXTEEN

DOGGIE TIME

Strict routines have me on a glide path to academic distinction in the late winter of my sixth-grade year. Go figure. I am one happy eleven-year-old boy. Not even the peskiest nun of the bunch is nipping at my heels any more—not since they put her away in a home. *Thank you, Lord.* Life is good and getting better. I'm playing basketball and pond hockey every day. Last fall I even made the football team.

With the powers that be desperate for warm blood, it seems that making the squad at St. Suzanne is solely dependent on your ability to turn your head and cough. After a weigh-in to make sure you don't exceed the 135 lb. limit, a member of our parish Booster Club rewards you with an extremely cool uniform. It makes you feel like a superhero when you ride your bike to practice in your pads. It's fantastic. There is just one thing more I need to make my life perfect. God knows I've earned it after a day like today. I got 100 on my math test, for God's sake. *Wait 'til Marge hears about that one.* Crossing the field, I can almost see sprigs of green sprouting beneath the thin expanse of crusty snow. It won't be long before baseball tryouts. Winter cold be damned. I'm in the mood to throw a ball against the house until my arm falls off. Then it hits me. Wouldn't spring be the perfect time of year to reward a hard-working boy like me with a puppy? Wouldn't it? *Geez-oh-Pete. Holy crap.* I am so excited, I sprint the rest of the way home. *C'mon, Lord, make it happen already, wudja?*

Most days, Marge is peeling potatoes when I walk through the door if she's not on the phone carrying out her duties as a sponsor. From her station at the sink, she is always at the ready with a slice of raw spud to hold me over until dinner as I download about school.

Something about this day is different. Marge isn't on the phone. And the potato peeler is nowhere in sight.

YES! Doggie-Doggie-Doggie-Doggie! It's really gonna happen. I have earned it. I will promise to feed it, walk it, train it, and groom it. I will love it to pieces. When it's thirsty, I will always be there for my little buddy. Always and forever. Swear to God, God. I swear to God. Thank you, Lord. Thank you.

Socks sliding on the linoleum, I slip and scramble, falling twice before finding my feet.

"Hey, settle down, buddy. Plant both cheeks here. We need to talk. I got some news."

Her words confirm what I've proudly known for a while. I have perfected the art of squirming! With that, I take my seat.

"Mikee, you are such a beautiful, handsome boy. You know I love you so very much."

I know...and you're proud of me, too...so we're getting a d.....?

"And you know that no one can one hundred percent predict the future, right? You know that, Mikee?"

Heck no, Mom. I am predicting that we're gonna get a doggie. We ARE getting a dog, aren't we?

"Well buddy, I went to the doctor a while ago..."

And the doctor's dog is gonna have a litter of puppies?

"... and I got a glimpse of the future."

And the puppies are expected when?

Deep breath. Marge sighs.

Geez. Come on, Mom. Get to the big news, already.

"I'm dying, Mikee."

"Huh?"

"I have a disease. It's something called Lymphosarcoma. That's a form of Leukemia. Honey, the doctor told me that I don't have long to live."

I don't even remember getting out of my chair when I find myself pressed against her. My tears are streaming. "How much time did they say we have, Mom?"

"Perhaps a year, maybe a little more, buddy. They can't be certain. I haven't yet told Patrick, but Kathy and Nino already know. I sat them down together, a few days ago." She drifts off, lost in thought.

"What the heck are we supposed to do now, Mom? What are we supposed to do now?" I can't stop holding on tight.

"Oh, my darling sparrow, God doesn't give many people an opportunity to prepare for death. But it seems He has given that gift to me. We'll just make the most of our time that's left. Okay?"

"'Kay."

"And let's pray for a miracle, shall we?"

"'Kay."

"Why don't you go out and throw a ball around, buddy. It'll make you feel better. I'll call you when it's time for dinner."

Dinner…what's dinner?

Nothing is making sense.

Hard as I try, it's impossible to swallow.

Out on the driveway the world spins around me.

I can't even grip a baseball.

I'm remembering now.

I was eleven when bewilderment stopped being my friend.

SEVENTEEN

A PROMISE OF THE UNIVERSE

Seven days pass and there are still no tears from Marge.

"This is no time to wallow," she tells us. "We've got too much to do."

She makes each of us promise that we will not share the news of her illness with anyone, especially since Patrick doesn't yet know.

Not a peep. Not to one soul. We promise.

I feel like I'm the one dying here.

Marge finds me in the kitchen.

"Hey. When you get knocked down playing football or hockey, what you do, buddy?"

"I get back up, of course, Mom."

"You sure do. We're a lot alike that way, aren't we?" Marge smiles.

"Uh-huh."

"Listen here. There's something you need to know, Mikee."

Oh, God, not again.

"Long after sports are behind you, you are still going to have plenty of knockdown moments in your life. Everyone does. So plan on it. You just need to treat them as opportunities to show God that you're strong enough to get right back up. Got it?"

"'Kay."

I bolt for the door. *Phew.* That was easy.

"Hey, hold on. Sit with me here a minute. Tell me something else. Do you know what the word *equilibrium* means, Mikee?"

"You mean balance?" I ask.

"That's right. Balance. Do you know that the universe is constantly seeking equilibrium?"

"Huh?"

"Well, you know about pendulums, right? When they swing, they always come back an equal distance the other way. And you know how the ocean's tides come in and go out. That's called ebb and flow. You know all about that, right?"

"Uh, huh."

"Well, those are all aspects of the universe at work, buddy. Listen. I know all this doom and gloom about my illness seems terrible to you now. But you have to believe that God has a plan for us. He wouldn't give you a burden that you couldn't handle. He knows you're strong, Mikee. Just remember, His universe will always seek balance. That's a promise."

Hopeless and clueless, I parrot her words. "Got it, Ma. The universe will always seek balance." All I really want to do is run away.

"Come here, kiddo."

She pulls me close. "Things seem scary, don't they?" she whispers.

"Uh-huh."

"But you've been afraid before and you've handled it. Do you remember when you were a little guy, afraid of the dark? Do you remember how your sister would sit on the edge of your bed and pat you on your back to help you fall asleep? Do you remember that?"

"Yup. I do, Mom. That's funny."

"Well, you've got to remember that tomorrow always brings a new day, buddy. And there is something else about the universe you need to know." About-face. She turns me toward her as she rests her wrists on my shoulders. "You need to know that after sad times, happy times follow. But it's not automatic. It takes some doing. The secret is to know how to make that happen." She is holding both of my hands now. "Listen up here. Happy times will follow sad times only if you let the bad things go, Mikee." She sounds serious.

"Huh?"

"Oh, I love you so much. You will always be my little sparrow, buddy, even though I know that you fancy yourself as some toughie. You cannot be angry and you cannot hold grudges just because life's currents seem to be working against you. Look at me. When something bad happens you have to shake your arms right down to your fingertips and let the anger go. Got it?"

"I think so."

"Here's the bottom line. If you're going to be successful and have a full life, focus on happy memories to build on. The positive stuff. That's what you need to hold onto deep in your heart, Mikee. But if you don't let the bad things go, the negative energy will take over and you'll reap what you sow in spades. Understand?"

"I think so. Sort of. Uh-huh." *Not really.*

"Aw buddy. There will be times when you will feel so bewildered it will make you mad. I know. You'll feel confused. It'll be just like that moment when the river meets the sea. Do you know what I'm talking about?"

"Huh?"

"Think about a river, Mikee. Think about how it flows calmly for miles. But when it meets the sea, there's absolute confusion. That's part of God's universe, as well. It's all part of His plan. Got it?"

Hearing her words makes me realize that I've never felt more confused in my life.

"Listen. As hard as it is to imagine, even the universe requires confusion at times. That's why the river swirls and crashes when it finally meets the sea. Because that is what it's meant to do, for a little while anyway, until it can make sense of the chaos. Then, it all works itself out and the river *becomes* the sea. Your challenge will be to get beyond those confusing currents, buddy. I know you can do it. Who knows you and who loves you?"

"You do?"

"You bet I do, buster. I'm counting on you now. You've got to make those currents work for you, not against you. And you've got to figure out how to hold onto the happy memories to build on. Okay? Do that for me, won't you? Hold those close in your heart. That's what makes life so interesting, actually. Figuring out which memories to keep and trusting that God has a plan is the secret of a full life. Got it?"

"Got it, Mom." *Not really.*

"Listen. God knows great challenges make great people, buddy. He knows what he's doing. Now, come here and give me a hug. We'll take a day at a time. Besides, your dad loves you and he will be here for you, long after I'm gone. You guys will all be just fine." She pulls me close. "You will always have your dad."

EIGHTEEN

DR. & MRS. CHURCH

AA has put Marge and Tony in touch with spheres of professionals whose interests and community standing extend far beyond the boundaries of our neighborhood. Among them, a prominent Detroit Psychiatrist, Dr. Aloysius Church, and his wife Elizabeth have become role models. Intellectual and spiritual stalwarts both, while some Detroiters know Elizabeth by her byline from occasional book reviews and art exhibit recommendations, Marge has come to know her as her best friend. They live in an upscale Westside subdivision called Rosedale Park with their three children, Al, Lizzie and Mike, all of whom are older than us.

They live on a corner lot on a street called Bretton Drive. A slate roof covers dormers on the upper story. A formal dining room sits next to a book-filled library near the foyer. Across a hall, the front room is loaded with treasures. There's a harp, violins, a saxophone, flutes and guitars. A grand piano fills an alcove near a bay window. They summer in Yarmouth, on Cape Cod. They winter in San Diego. They travel the world on business. And although their lives are vastly different from ours, the bond they form with Marge and Tony through AA cements their friendship.

It's been six weeks since I learned my mom was dying and I couldn't begin to understand why. On the heels of our conversation about equilibrium and the universe, I'm more bewildered than ever. Patrick is still oblivious to it all. Marge has arranged to spend tomorrow morning with him to break the news.

He and I are sitting together in "the way back" of our Bonneville station wagon. In Patrick-parlance, that leaves *Thing-One and Thing-Two* in the middle seat. Marge is shotgun as always, up front with our dad. Easter Mass has just ended. Dressed in our Sunday finest, we're on our way to the home of Dr. and Mrs. Church for an elegant brunch.

As soon as we walk through the door, Tony surprises us all by doing something he never once did at home, except on the occasion of Nino's tenth birthday. After removing his herringbone jacket, he tucks his tie into his dress shirt, rolls up his sleeves, and heads for the kitchen. Patrick and I follow. There's a towel knotted at his hip. A starched white apron is falling to his ankles.

Our dad has transformed into a chef.

Wielding a sharpening steel, he hones his blade to score a ham the size of a small medicine ball. In a glass bowl, he layers Vermont maple syrup with a dash of vinegar, a dollop of horseradish, a spatula of French mustard and some crumbles of brown sugar. After a vigorous whisk, he brushes the meat before dotting the centers of pineapple rounds with whole cloves all around the hock and placing it in the oven.

He trims and steams asparagus then bathes them for a minute in ice water with lemons swirling. Fanning the spears onto a platter, he squeezes a bit of juice on them, before shaving parmesan from a brick over the top. He covers the platter with foil and places it into a warming drawer. A wink from the chef gets a rise out Patrick. It evokes a tickled giggle. Our dad's pace is spellbinding.

Cooking to order for the adults, he whips up fluffy orange marmalade and Swiss cheese omelets, sprinkled with razor-thin scallions and a wisp of chive. For the kids, there are flaky croissants with apple-butter on the side, cinnamon-raisin twists, and soft-scrambled eggs. There's fresh-squeezed orange juice and milk out of crystal goblets. For Marge, there is coffee, black as coal, served in a fine bone-china cup with a traditional saucer, just as she likes it. At each place setting, a small pedestal holds a colored egg with each of our names stenciled on it. In the middle of each plate is a little gift, tied with a colorful ribbon.

It's a happy Easter.

As Tony attends to the final touches, Patrick and I shift on our stools. We're sitting next to a tall butcher-block prep table. The tumbled stone floor near the pantry makes our seats wobble. Mesmerized, we are watching our dad like hungry little hawks. Aside from never having seen him cook, I have never before heard him whistle either. Amazing. Lost in his craft, he begins talking about technique. It's almost enough to make me forget our mom is sick.

The flurry of brunch winds down. The adults adjourn to the library for a consultation. Marge gives direction as she pulls closed the double doors. "Kathleen, your dad and I need to speak to Dr. and Mrs. Church in private. Make sure everyone goes outside, will you? We need some alone-time together."

Hours pass.

None of us can remember our mom and dad having a longer conversation with anyone.

NINETEEN

THE TOLL

Dr. Church has insisted that communication take center stage, so Marge begins to download information to our dad. In the months that follow, week by week, she lays out the particulars of running the household. She shows Tony where she keeps our medical records. She explains how she uses the top drawer of our buffet in the dining room to organize bills and tax documentation. She shares her system for tracking our school activities. She shows him where she keeps clippings about sports and church events. He can't believe the number of envelopes filling that top drawer, beneath the label "bills to be paid."

Tony is gutted and inconsolable. He is drowning in despair. Where did *his* nirvana go? How is he supposed to raise these kids by himself? This wasn't the deal. Didn't he do everything that Marge asked? Didn't he give up the drink? Didn't he dutifully bring home his paychecks? Didn't he keep his hands off the kids and stay out of her way so she could raise them?

Wasn't that the deal, Marge?

Left unchecked, she realizes Tony's anger will tear us apart. She urges him to seek further counsel. "At least use Dr. Church for a referral, Tony. If you're not comfortable seeing our friend in a professional capacity, he can send you to someone to get help."

It's 1965, and "getting some help" can mean only one thing.

Calling Dr. Feel-good....

Marge has no choice but to become Tony's loyal enabler.

Of course, I'm clueless to it all.

My twelve-year-old heart only knows that I love my parents more than anything in the world. All I can do now is pray for a miracle, which makes me feel better, until I am overcome by a sinking feeling. For some reason I can't stop fearing that my words might become lost in translation.

Damn Devil.

For her part, Marge is determined to maintain a semblance of normalcy. She continues to share stories, and attend Mass, and go to Confession, and bag lunches, and shine our shoes and launder our shirts. She also continues with her duties as an AA sponsor, all the while keeping current on the bills by juggling household accounts, which is why our allowances take the form of non-monetary compensation, like watching *Saturday Movie Classics* on CBC, broadcast from across the river.

Marge joins us in the living room. With our dad at work or bowling, Kathy, Nino, Pat and I huddle under a blanket to watch *The Bishop's Wife*. It features a magnificent, lumbering St. Bernard named *Queenie* who steals the show from David Niven and a handsome angel named Dudley, with whom Marge appears smitten. She tries to mask it by sharing how tickled she is by Loretta Young, as I marvel to no one in particular, "Wow. Wouldn't it be cool to own a big doggie like that St. Bernard?"

To my surprise, it's Marge who first responds.

"You are so right, Mikee. That Queenie is one grand specimen. Who knows? Maybe we'll get lucky and have a dog as proud as that someday."

Huh?

Though far from a promise, if that day ever came, I knew Marge would enjoy having a dog like Queenie as much as anyone in the family.

If only she wasn't dying.

At Marge's insistence, Tony sticks to his own routines. He continues to spend summers cooking up on Black Lake.

Located in the northern section of *The Mitt*, the Maxon Agency's business retreat is where the ad executives entertain corporate guests all summer. They recreate all day. In the evenings, they enjoy fine dining before previewing the fall television lineups, watching shows like *Bonanza* to decide where to lock-n-load their advertising buys.

Tony doesn't talk much about it, other than to say that Time Magazine once did a story about that business retreat. According to the article, the Maxon Corporation's "*Cabin*" is a luxurious compound comprised of eleven buildings. There are tennis courts, stables, and overnight accommodations for up to seventy-two guests. When our dad isn't preparing his superb meals, he is on the lake fishing, most often with his good buddy and loyal second-in-command, who has the funniest name of anyone who has ever worked in a professional kitchen. He goes by *Piggy*. There is also a golf course nearby, which Tony enjoys, since everyone around can afford to wager.

It's the end of one of his long summer sojourns. I am planted on our porch for my dad's big arrival. I want to be the first one to see the doggie that I am sure he will bring home. I never say that out loud, though, for fear that I might jinx the moment that I have long imagined, when our car door opens and a little puppy comes tumbling out.

It's dark when he pulls in. He's holding something in his arms. "Hey kids, look what I found at a roadside stand!" he bellows.

Spinning, I fall to my knees. He presents us each with mass-produced beaded belts and feather headdresses. He tells us they were made in a teepee, by a tribe called "Onaway Indians."

Not quite what I was expecting.

I fear he's forgotten what I have been working so hard at school to earn. Gathering my courage, I approach him. I need to make sure he understands that my dream doesn't require a magnificent St. Bernard like that Queenie dog. Far from it. I am not the least bit choosey. A rescue puppy from the pound or a roadside stand would be perfect, as long as it's ours to keep, and care for and to call our own.

"C'mon, Mikee. Dogs are not cheap. What, are you stupid?" He lets that last word hang in the air. I can only stare. "What are you looking at?" he continues. "Do you think dogs grow on trees, Mikee? Hasn't anybody ever told you that nothing in life is free? Go ahead. Try to name one thing in life that's free. I dare you."

There's no way I'm going there; not after he's called me stupid.

As I turn to walk away, he adds a final embellishment, which I know isn't true. And with it he puts the matter to rest for good. "Besides, Mikee, I'm allergic to dogs. End of story."

Obsessing, I think about Marge's words from a few weeks before when she gave me the answer. *"It doesn't cost anything to dream, buddy. And here's the best part of all. God loves it when you dream. How cool is that? Dreams are free."*

Screw it.

Avoiding confrontation, I keep that nugget of wisdom to myself. There's no way he would have understood it, anyway.

Whenever we arrive with Marge at Sunday Mass now, handfuls of parishioners stand and gawk. Panicked by circumstance, our dad has made himself the victim. He's ignored our mom's wish that no one share the news of her illness with anyone outside the family. Given her subdued reaction to the murmurs, we begin feeling almost as sad about those whispers as we do about her condition.

For Marge, going to church becomes a daily event. Each morning at 6:15, she makes a solitary pilgrimage through the neighborhood to sit in her third row pew at 6:30 Mass.

Meanwhile, Tony is preoccupied with the arrangements for her funeral. Door-to-door, he secures commitments from other dads to carry her casket in the tradition of pallbearers. I am by his side at church one Sunday when he requests a *"Resurrection Mass for Marge."* Knowing that priests wear somber purple or black vestments for funerals, I am surprised to hear the monsignor's response. A vestibule full of parishioners take notice. *"Anything for Marge, Tony. Of course we'll wear white for her at her funeral. She deserves that and more."*

As for her grave marker, the granite has been cut. Lacking only an end date, it's ready for placement. There's also a caterer standing by to deliver a proper hot buffet to the house for visitors after her graveside service.

Months pass. The Marge-watch continues. Everyone in the neighborhood is on alert. Whispers now shadow her every move. Even strangers are inspired by her faith and stamina. Her sense of humor helps her cope. She cannot keep it in check. Friends talk about how the sound of her laugh lingers for days after their spending a bit of time together.

By month fifteen, people rush to hug her, always letting out big sighs when they do. She finds the attention embarrassing. It's the last thing in the world she wanted.

With all that's going on, my dad remains woefully unaware of my schedule. Can't blame him, really. Seasons come and go. Every time I have a game, I hope against hope that he'll show up. He doesn't. He's busy. When I ask him about it, he tells me to settle; that there will always be another game on another day; and that the best is yet to come. I can't imagine what could be better than having your own dad watch you play ball, or skate, or shoot hoops, or score a touchdown.

Maybe the next game.

I'm staring down a sign on the mound. I'm on the intermediate diamond across the short width of Faust from our house. I imagine my dad can see me. Ours is just one of sixty living room windows that surround that field, so it's impossible to know for sure if he might be somewhere nearby watching. It doesn't cost anything to dream. Right?

TWENTY

THE GOLDEN HAWKS

It's early October. I've risen to the rank of co-captain of the St. Suzanne Football Squad, such as it is. A ragtag but proud bunch of 125-pounders, they call us *The Mighty Golden Hawks*. It's a sorry joke. We more resemble a flock of skittish yellow parakeets on game days. Until last Sunday. We were ferocious. Winless the previous season, to our surprise, we finally won one.

"Hey, Mikee. Heads up." My favorite quarterback is yelling to his favorite fullback. "Check it out. Is that an ambulance? At your house? You better hustle."

Mom???!!!

Helmet still strapped on, I'm in a 400-yard dash from the practice field to the house in my high-tops. Laces flapping, sparks fly when I hit the concrete on Faust. *In the name of the Father...and of the Son....* The front door swings open. Sweat is pouring down my face. I am expecting to see Kathy. Maybe a priest.

Out steps Marge.

Thank you, God. Thank you.

I can't believe I made it home in time.

"Mom, Mom! Are you okay? One of the guys, Mark, he thought he saw an ambulance, I was sure—"

"Mikee, your dad had a heart attack. Honey, we've lost him."

Huh?

Just like everyone who knew and loved him, Tony never saw it coming.

TWENTY-ONE

THE ROSARY

A telephone table occupies the bottom of the stairs next to the tiny vestibule at our front door. Working with a flat, spring-loaded address book, Marge starts making calls. From my perch three steps up, it is obvious that she is talking to strangers. Secretaries, probably. Judging by her brief replies, *"Where's he being laid-out"* is all anyone is asking.

Telephone trees used to communicate school closings on "snow-days" spreads the news throughout the parish. The rest of the neighborhood learns of our dad's passing by word of mouth. Two nights later, mourners gather for Tony's Rosary.

It starts serenely.

Our eighth-grade and sixth-grade classes are first to arrive. A handful of nuns accompany the kids. Just as I had earlier pictured them, they gathered in our church parking lot before marching like a line of ducklings down Grandville to the funeral home on Joy. I also imagined the nun's shrill directions before they walked through the heavy doors. *"Lollygagging will not be tolerated, children."* Last to enter is the man who had volunteered to straggle behind to make sure no one strayed during the two-block trek from school, a *sweeper*, of sorts. Last in and last out, he makes a point of offering a kind word to both Patrick and me before slipping away himself. Those heartfelt condolences meant a lot coming from our school janitor, especially since we knew he was off the clock.

Next to arrive are Kathy's classmates from *Rosary*, the all-girl high school that she had graduated from the year before. They greet her with hugs. They remind her that they will be there for her. It's exactly the support Kathy so needs and deserves. Huddling as girls do, not one them went anywhere near the open casket, I noticed. It wasn't until a few neighbors began drifting in that we first heard the words, *"Oh, he looks so peaceful."*

Dr. and Mrs. Church arrive next with a contingent of AA faithful. Executives from the advertising firm and support staff follow. The PGA pro and his wife Cathy join, along with a group of meat, fish and produce purveyors, all of whom had known Tony for years. Looking very much like Jackie Robinson in his jacket and tie, our dad's pal Piggy came to pay his respects, as well. He's soon surrounded by a pack of seminarians who had come to support Nino.

Moments before the service, a group of men that I had never before seen came through the door. Long overcoats drape their shoulders. Silk ties, gold cufflinks and shiny shoes complete their ensembles. Rings on the smallest of their manicured fingers stand out as they clutch their rosaries.

Unlike other mourners, they give no time to small talk near the vestibule. Instead, they make a beeline for Marge. Pushing through the crowd, they seem to employ a sixth sense. Whenever they feel eyes upon them, they make a show of blessing themselves with the tiny crucifix at the end of their beads. They greet Marge with whispers of *"Ciao Bella,"* whatever that means. After kissing both of her cheeks, they take turns at the bier. Powder flies off the top of Tony's folded hands as they reach in to give them a squeeze. *Dear Lord in Heaven, it looks like they are trying to wake him.* On their way to the back of the room, each of them pauses to touch Patrick on his shoulder. One rubs the top of his head as he bravely tries to wipe away his tears.

Mission impossible.

All the while, Marge stands tall. Craning, she is gazing over the crowded room. I can't imagine how she must be feeling, looking out from beside a casket in a funeral parlor teeming with friends and loved ones. I wonder how many times over these past many months she's pictured this exact scene, perhaps floating over the room, observing from an entirely different perspective.

Aw, Mom.

Mother Mary, pray for us.

As the Rosary begins, I tell myself I am not to blame.

For the life of me, I can't figure out why I feel the way I do.

Throughout the evening, people I have never met stream calmly through the door, holding their hearts in disbelief and shrieking, "*Oh my God,*" when they spot our mom. Two of them faint. No one expects to see Marge standing in the front of that room. In the days before voicemail, most mourners thought they misunderstood the handwritten message when they read the words, "*Marge called Tony died.*" Even our parish priests, all of whom had received that same telephone note, expected to see Tony leading the Rosary and Marge in the casket.

Back home after the service, we are all relieved to have this night behind us.

The next day, the knock on our door came at noon.

Patrick has wandered over to the bowling alley to be with friends. Kathy is at work. Nino's gone back to Sacred Heart to find solace among the priests and his fellow seminarians. Marge and I are home alone when two of my four aunts arrive from Jackson. *No-shows* both at the funeral home the night before, at least they made it here today to be with Marge absent the crush of crowds. I figure that to be a good thing.

Marge felt terrible for our dad's widowed mom Mary who was about to bury her only son but she had not given these two sisters-in-law a moment's thought. Years before, they had made something clear. Since Marge had not been baptized into the Church as an infant, they believed her conversion to be something less than genuine. On her wedding day, they told her so. "*It's nothing but a sham,*" they said. She could never truly be part of their family, "*since you aren't a real Catholic,*" they told her.

Young Patrick reacted predictably when I told him that one, back when I first heard it. "*They were ta-talking about muh-mom not being a real cuh-Catholic? Get outta here. Really?*"

Really.

Years before, Marge had taken their full measure. I first heard about her misgivings when I was a tot. "*Those two sisters of your dad's are selfish and self-absorbed, Mikee, and they need our prayers.*" Of course, I hadn't a clue what she was talking about at the time. Regardless, on this day, I had to presume they had come to pay their respects to their dead brother's dying wife. Right?

I assumed wrong.

Respect had nothing to do with it.

They came on a mission. Without even a hello, they demanded that Marge hand over all of Tony's personal belongings. They insisted that they were entitled to his things rather than her, since she was dying, anyway. In the span of twenty minutes, their car was loaded with every one of his suits, shirts, ties, trousers, belts and shoes. They also found his collection of IZOD golf wear and straw hats, which he kept on a metal rack in the basement next to his golf clubs and his fishing rods, all of which found its way to their car, as well. They also took his cookware, his bone-handle carving knives, some hotel pans and an assortment of *Sheffield* cutlery. They even scarfed his chef's jackets; the ones that had his name embroidered on the pocket.

Throw them out, Mom. Just throw them outta here.

It wasn't to be.

"How can you let them do this, Mom? How can you let them take everything of dad's?" I had to know.

"They're just things, Mikee. At the end of the day, that's all they are."

In the midst of the chaos, she maintained her composure. "Take whatever you want," she told them, serene as she stood back with her arm around me to whisper, "The River is meeting the sea, buddy."

Huh?

They left with every worldly possession that Tony had, except for one. In the aftermath, I came across my dad's favorite book. *The Walter Hagen Story*, by *"The Haig, Himself."* Widely considered to be the greatest match play champion of all time, Tony's hero being Walter Hagen says a lot about the kind of man Tony wished he could be. The first American ever to win The British Open, Hagen went on to win four. In the process, Tony's favorite golfer became the brashest showman in the history of the sport, on his way to claiming five PGA Titles and two U.S. Opens. At least I had his book. Who needs a bunch of belts and shoes, anyway?

Although Marge would never tolerate sympathy, watching her measured reaction to the disgraceful behavior we witnessed that day made me feel sorry for her. Those two aunts of mine didn't even have the courtesy to say goodbye after leaving our house a ransacked mess. I'd never felt more angry about anything in my life.

"We need to pray for them, Mikee."

"Huh? *Us*? Pray for *them*? Are you kidding me, Mom?" *The nerve.* I wanted to take somebody's head off. How could they insult Marge that way, in my presence? I *so* wanted to crush someone.

"That's right, Mikee. All we can do is pray for them. Listen up here. If anyone needs our prayers, it's those two. Believe me. Someday they will be found out for what they are. Do you remember what I told you about the universe and equilibrium? God will take care of this. There's nothing for us to do. I'm sorry you had to see that, honey."

Closing her eyes, she shakes her arms right down to her fingertips in an attempt to show her angry eighth-grader how to let a very sad, very bad thing go.

This, I will never get over.

TWENTY-TWO

BOB & CLAIRE

Marge's mom and dad are a joy whenever they visit our home. Born in Cork as Claire O'Ceary, Mrs. Robert Denny sings and laughs often. Her husband Bob is a storyteller supreme who most enjoys sharing tales about famous and not-so-famous racehorses. Holding court in front of the bricked-in fireplace of their one-bedroom flat near Dexter and Grand River, he expounds on his prized collection of *thoroughbred miniatures* that grace his mantle. Exquisite ivory, bronze or fine alabaster, I figure. Sometimes, he even allows me to hold one, but only when we are together. And whenever I do, he tells me about epic races involving horses with mysterious names and the offspring they sired.

Hungry to hear the lilt in his voice, which makes me so very happy, I pose a question, unsure if he has an answer. "Why do they call it the Sport of Kings, Gramps? What's that all about?"

He pauses.

"It's all about holding onto your dreams, laddy." He grins as he hands me one of his prized possessions from his mantle, which I am surprised to discover is thin hollow plastic.

"As hard as I work," he continues, "when I am in the heel of the hunt, and my horse is in the running, even *I* feel like a King, I do, even though the loykes of us could never expect to meet one of d'em. Not in a million years would we find ourselves standing in the same room. It matters not. That's something most folks could never expect to do, anyway. Oh, but standing tall at the rail, *feeling* like royalty, with a winner in moy pocket…that's plenty close enough for me, Moykee." His voice trails. "…and maybe for both of you, too, one day."

He winks at Patrick and then pulls him close as he gives us each a hug.

At six-two, our grandfather Bob is a blistered, Belfast-born *Orangeman*, as lean as he is Protestant. Thin as a rail, with a full head of white hair, he's never raised his voice in anger. Except once. His exasperation made Patrick and me both think that the roof of their flat had caved in when we heard him scream the word "*WHUT?*"

Marge had asked her mom to meet her downtown for lunch, as a ruse. All in accordance with her plan, they began their little adventure at Grand Circus Park, before strolling down Washington Boulevard. Upon arriving at St. Aloysius, Marge had a surprise for her mother. A priest was waiting inside the heavy doors to perform a simple blessing with holy water. By receiving those sprinkles, Marge told her mom that it constituted a baptism.

"It was something I just felt I needed to do," Marge shared with us later.

If our grandfather harbored any doubt about whether his daughter was headstrong when it came to her faith, he did no longer. It took a little time, but after a wee bit of raised blood pressure, the matter of Claire's surprise induction into the Church of Margaret Mary passed by the wayside without incident.

Bob loved his bride and he loved his family, made evident by his commitment to provide during the Depression. At the end of the *Roaring Twenties*, he stopped working in the Pennsylvania coalmines to move his family to Detroit, where he landed a job at the Ford Rouge Plant. For a line-worker like Bob, *The Rouge* was the place to be. In time, Charles Sheeler would memorialize its smokestacks in paintings. His assembly-line workplace would gain further prominence as the subject of muralist Diego Rivera, whose images still grace the walls of the Detroit Institute of Arts. Now, Bob has earned a gold watch. On its back it's inscribed with the Ford Motor Company logo below the words,

"1933 – 1961...*To Robert Denny...For Faithful Service.*"

The feast of St. Patrick means big hugs and mushy kisses the moment our grandparents come through the door. Claire completes the tradition when she takes control of the kitchen to make "*real Irish food*" for dinner. Cabbage and boiled potatoes with sprinkles of Durkee's Parsley from a tin would comprise the feast. Deprived of the pleasure of corned beef until later in life, we never had reason to complain since our house was filled with song and laughter on those occasions. The best part was seeing just how proud Marge was to be our mom when our grandparents came over for a celebration.

Those visits ended around the time of my ninth birthday. Marge and Tony were both pictures of health, living the dream on Faust. By 1962, Bob and Claire were able to realize their own dream when they moved from Detroit to Florida to reside in a simple motel room, next door to the flocks of flamingos on the infield at Hialeah Park, where our grandfather found his nirvana.

In the years leading up to their move, Grams would come over to babysit for Patrick and me while our mom ran errands. Our routine was set in stone. While she made our grandfather's chocolate peanut butter fudge from his secret recipe, Patrick and I would entertain ourselves by pushing our tushes into stainless steel bowls to spin on the linoleum floor. Our goal was simple; get dizzy enough to stand up and fall down.

Once her fudge found the oven, Claire would adjourn to the living room with a box of Kleenex to watch her favorite TV show. It had something to do with young mothers telling stories about their wretched lives—like having children with polio or husbands who were alcoholics. When a "winner" was crowned, Claire would begin to blubber as they presented the "queen" with a long golden scepter, a dozen roses, a new kitchen appliance and sometimes even a pair of crutches for having shared the most dismal real-life story in the history of depressing afternoon television.

"Are you okay?" Claire hollers through her tears. "You boys okay in there?"

"Fine, Grams. We're fine," I assure, while Patrick spins.

Cue the barf bag.

"Here cuh-cuh-comes lunch, mu-Mikee," he is proud to announce.

Our grandmother's curious allegiance to that *Queen for a Day* program made for a poignant conversation in late February of 1964 when Marge had to place a call to Florida. Without a trace of self-pity, she shared the diagnosis from her doctor. "Stay positive for me, Mom. The news isn't good, but we'll pray. That's all we can do. It's in God's hands. Believe me, I am staying positive. Okay? Don't you worry about me. It could be worse, you know. At least these kids will have their father after I'm gone."

Not.

TWENTY-THREE

A MIRACLE

In the months following our dad's funeral, Marge strengthens her resolve by making use of something she refers to as her *Security Charge Card*. It underwrites a Christmas for the ages. Except for survivor's benefits from Social Security and a modest Lincoln Life Insurance Policy to pay for her own funeral expenses, Marge exists on Kathy's minimum wage from the neighborhood grocery and that charge card.

"The balance owing is insured. It will be paid-off when I die. Just say a prayer the issuer of this little piece of plastic doesn't find out I've got one foot out the door, will ya? See this, Mikee. That's my name on it, right? I plan on using this little bugger until I drop, thank God."

Christmas Eve brings Nino home from the Seminary just in time to watch me serve Midnight Mass to an overflow congregation at St. Suzanne. Afterwards we keep with tradition. We all go straight to bed. Marge gets busy.

The next morning, our tree is aglow and it's covered in silver tinsel, where there was none the night before. Bing Crosby's *White Christmas* sets the tone. Wrapped packages cover the floor, more than ever before. Marge has gone all-out. And even though the boxes contain practical gifts like handkerchiefs, socks and underwear, whenever we tear through the wrapping, we respond like she has just given us the keys to a new Cadillac. We also find dress shirts and trousers nice enough to wear to school.

Stationed at our mom's side, Kathy picks up wrapping paper as Marge makes a final pronouncement. She tells us all to hang tight for a minute. There is one more present from Santa. "Turn up the stereo, Mikee, I'll be right back."

The screen door slams. The music is joyous. Marge reappears carrying a puppy. It's a beautiful gray-and-white Old English sheepdog. We reach immediate consensus. The new addition to our family will be called "*Duchess*," we agree. *Oh, my God.* She is soft and sweet, and she cuddles like a champion. She is everything I had ever hoped for in a puppy.

Kathy's reaction is pure. She giggles like a schoolchild. It's obvious to me that Marge wants her to feel like she will soon be in charge of a *real* family, with a beautiful shaggy dog and all. I can't believe it. Getting a dog was the last thing in the world I expected on this morning. But now that we have Duchess, maybe everything will work out fine, just like in the movies.

"How about our little *shake-a-fannie*? Have you noticed our Duchess doesn't have a tail so she just waggles her butt? Oh, what a beauty! I'm so glad you like her. And I love the royal name you gave her, guys. You know, this is the kind of doggie that the Queen of England would be delighted to own. Oh, you kids deserve her. Duchess is going to love being a part of our family." Her voice trails as our six-week-old beauty follows Marge into the kitchen. Right on cue, Duchess waddles near a corner of newspaper that Marge had set in front of the sink. She squats to pee, but misses. "Oh…good effort, little one. Good effort, honey. Good girl," Marge praises. "That's why God invented sheet linoleum, Mikee."

Her laughter fills the room.

Christmas night. For the first time in my life, I find myself in bed with the glorious scent of puppy breath all over me. Nothing ever smelled so sweet. With little Duchess breathing in and breathing out, I am dead to the world as soon as my head hits the pillow…

…*We are standing on an expansive green lawn before the Queen of England. She is sitting with a brood of puppies by her side. Dressed in yellow, head-to-toe, the Queen is wearing an enormous wide-brimmed hat. As we approach, Marge takes the lead. "How do you do, Your Majesty," she says with a slight bow. "Allow me to present my son Mikee."*

"How do you do, Master Mikee," the Queen replies. "I am here to present you with something, too, kind sir."

At that moment, the Queen reveals a beautiful Old English sheepdog puppy on a glittering leash. "Her name is Duchess, Mikee. Take good care of her…."

The next morning I tell Marge all about it.

"Do you dream in color, Mom?"

"Every once in a while, I do. I must admit it's rare, but it's always magnificent when it happens."

"Aw, Mom. My dream last night, it was in color! You were in it, too, and so was the Queen of England. We met the Queen, Mom. You and me. There were Palace guards and everything."

"Queen Elizabeth? You and me? We met her? Oh, Mikee!" She laughs. "Well, now that I think about it, I shouldn't be surprised. From everything I've read, the Queen loves doggies as much as you do, buddy, although a dream like that one would make your grandfather laugh out loud, I'll tell you. Hold onto that pipedream for me, would you?" She says it with a giggle as she tickles my armpit.

It feels good to laugh at the absurdity of it all.

Having Duchess in the family makes me feel like a miracle has happened. It's as if Marge is no longer dying. Everything is going to be okay.

Where there was once sadness and uncertainty, there is now jubilation on Faust every morning.

At last, we had our dog.

Marge is as happy and proud as we have ever seen her.

TWENTY-FOUR

FIT FOR A QUEEN

It's late May. Kathy is making a trip to visit our grandparents in Florida. It will mark the first time she has ever been on an airplane. It will also be the first vacation of her young life. Bob and Claire can't wait to see her.

While she is away, Duchess is diagnosed with severe hip-dysplasia. We learn it is not at all uncommon for large, popular purebreds. The vet blames it on excessive inbreeding. Our beautiful little one is in excruciating pain. Deteriorating fast, she can no longer get up and move around, even to relieve herself.

Marge instructs me to take us to see the vet. At her insistence, I'd obtained my learners permit the month before when I became the youngest Driver's Ed student in the history of Cody High. Now still way shy of lawful driving status, I am about to embrace my role as Marge's full-time chauffeur.

"Is this legal, Mom?"

"If I say it's legal, it's legal. Don't worry about it. Come on. Let's get going."

Duchess is lying on the back seat. Marge is all business as she takes a moment to prepare me. She can't be certain, but it is possible we will have to put Duchess down, she cautions.

The consultation takes fifteen minutes. The news is not unexpected.

Marge excuses herself. I assume she has gone into the business office to negotiate payment arrangements. When she doesn't return right away, I lean over the reception counter. There, I hear a conversation that is growing heated. Fearing that Marge's magic charge card might be acting up, I make my way into the back.

She and the doctor are in an examination room. Our puppy is lying on a tall metal table, on her side, staring straight ahead. I rush to give Duchess a kiss. God love her. Marge is stroking her belly, finishing a sentence. "...over her grave."

The vet looks incredulous. "Excuse me?"

"I said that we have to bury our puppy and say a proper prayer over her grave," Marge repeats.

He shakes his head. "Ma'am, we have procedures and I am afraid that is not one of them."

I have never seen her more insistent.

The shovel is longer than I am tall. I found it in a utility closet next to a mop basin. Outside the vet's back door, I find a solitary patch of grass behind a short row of commercial buildings. Marge joins me a few minutes later. Inside, an attendant is wrapping Duchess in a small body bag. The vet carries her out and places her in the hole that I dug. After I smooth the last bit of dirt over the burial ground with the edge of the shovel, Marge takes my hand. Standing on her other side, our flabbergasted vet does the same. Heads bow. Marge says two simple prayers over the small mound of dirt. It's a grave fit for a Queen.

Kathy returns a week later. Although she and Marge had talked on the phone, she knows nothing about Duchess. Marge would never spoil her big trip. She knows how much Kathy loves our beautiful puppy.

On the ride to the airport, Marge shares a plan with Patrick and me. We will meet Kathy at her gate. We will take her to a coffee shop within the terminal. Once seated, she tells us, Marge will share the news that Duchess is no longer with us.

I drop them at the main terminal. After parking the car, I spot Patrick a few paces inside the automatic entry doors. He is alone.

"Mom took off. That way," he says as he points. "Some kind of commotion. She told me to wait here."

People are rushing in every direction. Marge is nowhere in sight. Then, I spot her. She is on her hands and knees at the bottom of an escalator. She's helping a lady who looks like a runway model from an auto show whose stocking is caught in the teeth of the machinery. Working with small cuticle scissors, Marge frees the woman, as a stream of passengers push their way past them. I help her to her feet. The stranger hugs her. Marge the statuesque beauty now appears tiny and frail.

The stranger speaks. "How can I ever thank you?"

Marge smiles. "I'm just glad you're okay."

"But how can I thank you?" the woman asks again. By her accent she might be from Paris. Montreal perhaps. She reaches for her purse. Marge takes her arm to hold it still.

"Just remember me in your prayers, dear," Marge tells her.

"I will. I will," the woman insists. "At least tell me your name."

"I'm Marge, honey. I'm glad you're ok. Safe travels."

"You are my savior, Marge."

With a peck on both cheeks and a final thank you, the beautiful lady in open-toe shoes with the hole in her stocking hurries down a busy concourse to catch her flight. "*Je ne peux pas dire assez à vous remercier, Marge.*"

Marge beams like she understands every word.

She is still beaming as Patrick comes strolling along like he owns the place. As we approach the gate, she stops us in our tracks. She grabs us each by an ear. "OK, guys, do not forget. We are going to greet your sister at the gate and we are going to take her to the coffee shop. Got it? That's where I will share the news about Duchess, calm and deliberate. Do you understand what I am saying?"

She is *not* foolin' around.

"Got it, Mom." To reinforce our understanding, we nod in unison. When she sees our chins hit our chests at the same time, she acknowledges with a simple "Good."

This is not going to be easy.

Kathy comes off the plane, radiant. She is running toward us. She is tan and beautiful. Marge gives her a big hug, as do I. Swept up in the moment, Patrick is unable to contain himself. "Hi Kathy, the dog's dead."

Marge catches him clean. A swift cuff to the back of his head makes her twelve-year-old squeal.

"Ouch! What was that for, Ma?"

The next day, as soon as Kathy heads into work, Marge instructs me to drive her to the puppy store. "I need to talk to the guy that sold me our dog...in person."

I am so glad I am not him.

TWENTY-FIVE

WELCOME TO PUPPY PALACE

Marge maxed out her charge card when she bought Duchess, dreaming that a dog of size and pedigree might help to keep us feeling like a family after she was gone. We later learned that the store where she bought our dog was known all over town as a "puppy factory," a mill that bred more disgruntled patrons than healthy dogs. It was, however, accessible by public transportation, a major consideration for Marge.

She took the Greenfield bus to Eight Mile Road on that December 24th so she could surprise us with a Christmas to remember. I try to picture her trip home and what it must have been like for her to travel that day with a little sidekick like Duchess. It's impossible to imagine how many new friends they must have made.

Nearing the store, she tells me that she is anticipating a *"no returns"* policy, even though Duchess hadn't lived six months. "I'm prepared for that. Don't worry, Mikee. Just keep your wits about you and watch me. I'll handle this."

Marge will demand a refund, or a new dog. No doubt about it. The bill from the vet is in her purse, right next to the receipt from her big purchase on Christmas Eve. She is in no mood to hear about store policy.

The manager is insistent. "Lady, we don't give refunds of any kind, period. Now, get out of my store."

Easy, Mister. Whoa there, fella...do you have any clue who you are dealing with here?

It's obvious that this guy didn't.

Even with her failing health, this little schmuck wouldn't stand a chance if Marge decided to take him down with one of her mighty swats. That much I knew firsthand. *Go ahead, Mom. Whack that little shite! Take him down good. Our dog is dead, for God's sake. If anyone deserves a good smacking, it's this guy.*

It feels good to be on the other side of the fence for a change.

Without a fuss, we leave the store. When we get to the car, I ask her why she didn't smack that obnoxious manager and take him down.

"That's another perfect example, Mikee, of when you cannot hold onto feelings like that. You have got to lose them. Do you hear me? You need to shake your arms right down to your fingertips and just let that anger go. Got it?"

"I got it, Mom." I don't believe a word of it.

"Trust me. I have a plan," she tells me.

She orders me to drive to a nearby school supply store. After we pick up materials for a future science fair presentation, I am convinced that we are going to head back home to live without a dog forever. *Damn.* I can't believe it. Where is the mom that used to chase me around the garage? Where is that old fighting spirit? Where the hell is *that* Marge, the one we all know and love?

Ten minutes later, her plan is revealed.

Equipped with poster board and markers, she makes a sign on the hood of the car, and then places it face down on the back seat, in the exact spot Duchess laid the day before.

"Take me back to that puppy store, Mikee. Pronto."

Whoa. Did she say "pronto"?

"No problem, Mom. We'll be there in a jiff." In my heart I'm hoping she's going to walk back in and smack that little doofus.

Letting go is not easy.

I park in the adjacent lot. Marge retrieves her sign. In a radical contradiction to her sense of dignity, she holds it over her head as she paces back and forth, up and down busy Eight Mile. The poster says it all.

PUPPY PALACE
UNFAIR TO DYING MOTHER
HONK!

Vehicles crawl. Fists pump. Horns blare. The one thing missing are television news crews.

A short while later, the manager appears. Standing in the front of his store on the eastbound side of the street, he pleads, "Lady, you are making a spectacle. I beg you. Please stop this, immediately."

Marge keeps pacing.

"Look."

With that one word, she has his full attention.

"I will stop only if you give me cash or another dog, right now. I mean it, buddy. I will stay here all night, if I have to. I kid you not. My family needs a dog and we need one today."

Whoo Hoo! You go, Mom!

With wash from a traffic-copter overhead, the manager nods in agreement. And with horns still honking, the two head back into the store.

"Just stand over there, Mikee, and be quiet. Oh, yeah, I forgot. Say a prayer for this guy not to check that charge card balance," she whispers. "I'm serious. Say a prayer. Now."

Enter our St. Bernard puppy.

Named after a Michigan State Defensive End, little Bubba would become a lumbering specimen, as proud and magnificent as *Queenie* from *The Bishop's Wife*. Forever a puppy at heart despite his mass, sighing and snoring under the kitchen table at Marge's feet becomes his favorite pastime. It wouldn't take long before that heavy table would begin lifting from the floor and float over toward his water bowl whenever he awoke from a nap. A grand master of eye contact, head tilts, tail wags and face licks, Bubba makes my first year of high school pass in a flash. Even Algebra I is tolerable, though no less difficult. With Bubba around, life feels like one big happy cartoon.

Before long, our mister magnificent is towering over the shoulder-high gate that leads to our backyard, raising a holy fuss to scare the bejeezus out of strangers who approach. Bubba knows who is who. With friends, he is always love-struck.

TWENTY-SIX

CAMELOT

It's the beginning of my sophomore year of high school. *Camelot* is playing on the stereo every morning now. Enjoying her coffee and a book, Marge manipulates her feet on the belly of her favorite footrest. Bubba is snoring away as Robert Goulet croons, "*If ever I would leave you, how could it be in springtime....*"

Marge tells me that she wants a little tape deck at the hospital when she goes in for her next round of tests so she can listen to music bedside.

"You bet," I tell her. I'm half-listening. At this stage, my mind is wandering all over the place. I have hit a wall of denial. After all, Marge *has* defied the predictions of all of her doctors and medical experts so far. I'm hoping she might be getting better. I'm also glad that I have a ride to school on this morning, since it will give Marge and me a few extra minutes at the kitchen table before the car horn sounds in the driveway.

"Trust your instincts, Mikee," she begins.

"Huh?"

"I said, trust your instincts. You have good ones, so use them."

"Sure, Ma."

"Hey, did I tell you about the quote I found from my maestro? Listen to this. *'To achieve great things, just two things are needed; a plan, and not quite enough time,'* she says as she giggles. "Isn't he fabulous? Do you know what I pray for every morning at Mass, Mikee?"

"What's that, Mom?"

"I just pray that we'll have enough time."

All of a sudden, I don't feel like leaving. Marge fast-forwards into my future. "When you are old enough to be blessed with children, buddy, I have no doubt that you will be the father of boys. You are such a boy. You are gonna have sons of your own. I'm sure of it."

Beep-beep.

I am off.

A month of kitchen-table Mondays pass. Each morning Marge and I sit together as a dreamy Bubba licks her toes. "I think that's why my feet are retaining water," she offers, smiling wide. It's a Saturday morning.

Not quite audible, *Camelot* plays in the living room.

Kathy is at work. Patrick is a few blocks away at his home-away-from-home, Crown Lanes, where he has begun working the shoe counter on weekends. Nino is where he always is, at the Seminary, of course.

"Let's chat, shall we?" Marge is in a mood to share. "Mikee, did I ever tell you how much I used to love wearing red fingernail polish?"

Huh? Of all the things that we could be talking about, Marge wants to chat about fingernail polish? I took the bait.

"Oh really, Mom, red fingernail polish? Hmmm...."

Marge has beautiful hands and the prettiest clear fingernails you could imagine. I'd never once seen anything but clear polish on her nails.

"Yeah, really," she continues. "I thought you knew, Mikee, that I gave it up, red fingernail polish, when I gave up the drink." Then she reminds me for the umpteenth time that she stopped boozing during her pregnancy with Patrick. "I'm quite proud of that. I was able to figure out a simple way to remind myself every morning that I needed to take one day at a time if I was going to lick my problem. That was not the easiest thing to do, you know."

"Giving up the drink?" I offer, knowing what she wants to hear.

"No, that part was easy, Mikee," she giggles. "The hard part was giving up the red fingernail polish!"

Oh God, it feels good to laugh with Marge.

Confused by the commotion, Bubba lifts his head before letting out a big sigh and rolling onto his side. Such a massive, docile beast he is.

"Here, Mikee. I want you to have something. It's my AA medallion. Take it. Keep it for me, okay? Years from now, I hope it will remind you of that little laugh we just had together." She pulls me close. "Oh, my darlin' sparrow, do you know how vain I am?"

"Huh? What do you mean, *vain*, Mom?" I haven't a clue.

"Well, here's the deal. I don't think I can bear to have people stare at me with maudlin funeral home makeup all over my face when you do the Rosary. And I've lost an awful lot of weight. I just think it would be better for everyone if we had a closed casket. Do you know what that means? It means I want you to be in charge. Okay? I want you to take control. Handle all of it. Have the casket opened for a private viewing for Bob and Claire when they arrive from Florida, but not for anyone else. No one else, Mikee, do you understand what I'm saying?" Marge is serious.

"I understand, Mom. I understand."

"One more thing. Your sister will be in no condition to choose a casket. Do not make Kathy do that. Do you think you and Nino can handle it and eliminate her involvement altogether?"

"No worries. We'll handle it."

"Good boy. Just keep your sister out if it. Handle that casket business for me. Pick out the cheapest one, all right?"

"Okay."

"I will always love you, Mikee, and I'll always be praying for you. Be strong for me."

At that moment, if she had asked me to commandeer a raft and paddle across the Atlantic, I'd have tried. "I will, Ma. I'll be strong."

"Mikee, we need to avoid an emotional meltdown here. The funeral home is going to be a nut house. A lot of people are going to want to be involved. Some will try to stick their noses where they don't belong, so we've got to do this thing right. Okay? You have to be decisive. That's why I'm giving you specific directions. Do you understand?"

"I understand."

"You are one of a kind, my sparrow. Don't forget. Happy times will follow sad times only if you let the bad things go. Just let 'em go, okay?"

"'Kay."

"And don't ever forget how much I'll always love you. I know how hearing that makes you happy. Hold that in your heart for me forever, would ya?"

"Of course, Mom."

Looking into her eyes, I see something I never before could have imagined. Marge is crying. Before I can even take a breath, we are weeping together.

Nothing ever felt so right.

"There's something else, Mikee."

Our breaths skip.

"Don't let a day go by without telling your sister you love her. Promise me," Marge insists.

"I promise, Mom."

Marge has never asked me to promise her anything.

"Every day. Tell her you love her. Work hard. Make your sister proud. Got it?"

Marge knew how to keep it simple. It's just like the way she used to caution me, back when I first started school. *"Grades are irrelevant, just behave, mister. Good conduct is what's important."* Her enlightened approach resulted in almost effortless academic success for each of us. And whenever I came home with straight As, she always replied, *"Isn't that terrific, you got an 'A' in conduct. Good work."* Then, we would celebrate with cupcakes for dessert after dinner.

She is looking deep in my eyes as she holds onto my hands. "Remember, God loves it when you dream, Mikee. It won't be long now. In a short while, you'll be doing the dreaming for both of us, won't you? Just keep in mind that I'll be praying for you, every step of the way. There's nothing you can't do, buddy, as long as you work hard, play the game fair, and love and respect your sister. Do that and all of our dreams will come true."

I want to believe it more than anything.

"And take good care of Bubba for me. If anyone deserves a dog as grand as this one, it's you, mister."

She leans down to stroke his magnificent belly. Bubba responds with another deep sigh and a long happy stretch across the width of our small kitchen floor. When Marge sits up he resumes licking her toes.

"Mikee, a couple more things."

"Huh?"

"Don't take a second mortgage out on the house."

"Got it, Mom. I won't take a second mortgage out on the house." I have no idea what she means but I am not about to interrupt her flow. There will be time to figure that out later.

"Oh yeah, there's something else. Do me a favor, will you?"

"Sure, Mom. Anything."

"Don't let your sister date cops."

Huh?

"You were named after an Archangel, Michael. Be Kathy's angel on that one."

"Got it, Mom."

No disparagement intended. I understood her concern. Marge just wants what's best for Kathy. First responders of all stripes, more than a few of whom live nearby, had become scarred by events of the previous summer when rioting tore our city apart. I got yanked from a baseball scrimmage over at Northwestern High on that hot July Sunday when it all began. A city Fire Chief, one of our neighbors and the owner of that magnificent boxer *Duke*, rolled out onto the field just after 2 o'clock that afternoon. *"Damn it, Mikee. What are you doing here? We are under curfew. Effective immediately. All of you. Get your asses home. Now. Tell your mothers they can thank me later."*

Just like the blind pig on 12th and Clairmount busted hours before eighteen blocks away, our game ended in abrupt fashion as well. Now, looters are tossing Molotov cocktails. Pedestrian-snipers are populating rooftops. Facing attack from gunfire, city firefighters are risking their lives to contain the first of 2,000 blazes not far from the vicinity of Sacred Heart Seminary on West Chicago and Linwood, where Nino resides. President Johnson is working with Governor Romney. They are preparing to direct thousands of U.S. Army and National Guard Troops to assist city law enforcement.

Making my way home, I see the clear blue sky over West Grand Boulevard is becoming shrouded in thick black smoke. Tactical Mobile Units, known in our neighborhood as TMUs, are roaming Grand River. Sirens are screaming. By week's end, even the 82nd Airborne would see action. After five days of mayhem, more than 1,100 were injured, 7,000 were arrested and 43 people were dead.

For most of those hired to protect and serve, it was impossible to leave work behind, so they carried it with them twenty-four-seven. Who could blame them? Since Marge's one and only daughter had been befriended by an undercover STRESS cop who lived in the neighborhood, Marge was just asking me to do whatever I could to keep Kathy from becoming a casualty, too.

That much I understood.

TWENTY-SEVEN

PROVIDENCE

It began in uneventful fashion, that Saturday afternoon. Kathy, Nino and Pat had been with Marge at the hospital since early in the morning. They spent the majority of their time being responsive to her requests to help her keep track of her white blood cell count. Each time they did, she would scribble down a little note onto a small bookie pad that she kept next to her bed. She became obsessed with that.

I had spent that morning and afternoon running errands with Lee from next-door, stocking up on supplies for his long-planned family trip to a lake up north. As soon as we arrived at the marine supply store on Telegraph in Dearborn Heights, they handed me a message marked URGENT. It directed me to go to Providence Hospital.

With his fresh-minted driver's license in his pocket, Lee drove me straightaway. I told him to drop me off.

It's three o'clock. As soon as I walk onto Marge's floor, Kathy, Nino and Pat head down to the cafeteria to grab a bite of food. They had not taken a break since early that morning.

Now, Marge and I are alone, oxygen tent and all. The scent of sacred oils linger. A candle burns at bedside. The room smells of Last Rites. From beneath the plastic, she takes my hand. She whispers through labored breaths, "Hold… happy…memories...love your daughters…for me."

My mind scrambles to understand her meaning. Marge and I had long ago agreed that if I were so blessed, I would be the father of boys, of course. The meds must be taking over. God love her.

God bless her.

A few days before, I brought a small tape deck to the hospital, as she had requested. Marge kept it on the stand next to her bed. A soft croon is filling the room. After a succession of Camelot-filled mornings leading up to this moment, I feel like I am hearing that song for the first time.

"If ever I should leave you, how could it be in — "

"Change…it."

"Huh?"

"Pas…de…Deux."

Her Nutcracker tape is already queued. Tchaikovsky fills the room. The tent contracts when she takes her last breath. It's the thirtieth day of March. It's springtime.

Kathy, Nino and Patrick return.

We hold hands. We cry. We pray.

Priests and nuns mingle in the hall.

Hospital personnel begin to gather.

TWENTY-EIGHT

CORNINGWARE AND PYREX

I'm too exhausted to argue after Nino ditched me at the funeral parlor two hours ago. Arriving home, I find our kitchen table overflowing. With news of Marge's passing, mothers all over the neighborhood have begun baking pies and every kind of casserole you can imagine.

Despite those generous gestures, Patrick is not a happy camper. LBJ is interrupting his television viewing with an announcement. He will not be seeking re-election. Marge would have viewed that as good news. She supported Senator Robert Kennedy's candidacy, believing that his election would end the war. While her devotion to JFK was all about style and cultural pride, with Bobby it was all about heart.

A line forms out our front door in the days that follow as a parade of moms and children queue-up with armfuls of wonderful food. They always leave empty-handed. White Corningware loaf dishes with blue cornflower designs are stacked next to Pyrex pie plates on the counter. Trays of goodies fill the fridge.

Bubba takes on Marge's persona from the past few months. He never once raises a fuss. Calm and somber, he greets everyone who comes through the door with a gentle bow, pushing his crown into their knees. Children laugh. Most don't want to leave. They all want to take our big boy home. Despite the weighty matters at hand, Bubba displays magnificent composure. He sets a superb example for us all.

When the house clears, we adjourn to the dining room, Kathy, Nino and me. It feels a bit strange to sit at that table without our parents.

I take a deep breath.

Kathy begins. She tells us that she got through to Bob and Claire in Florida. They are on their way.

"They're driving, right?" I ask.

"Of course they're driving, Mikee. You know your grandfather and his Irish superstitions. He wouldn't get on a plane if his life depended on it. *'If the pilot's time is up, I'm not the least bit interested in going down with him,'* he's said so often."

It feels good to laugh. So far, so good.

"How about his reaction if a chair tipped over when someone got up from the table?" I add. "That was a good one."

"Oh… and spilled salt." At long last, Nino speaks. "Over the left shoulder with it, immediately!"

Kathy giggles. "How about his insistence that he always leave the house by the same door he entered? Oh, my gosh, you should have seen him on the afternoon when he almost stepped out the wrong door."

"So when *can* they be here, Kath?" I ask.

"Late Tuesday? Maybe? Let's say Wednesday morning just in case, Mikee."

"Got it," I tell her. "That shouldn't hold up the Rosary, right? They'll miss it. But I'm sure that would be fine with Bob," I add.

"Ya think?" Kathy smiles. "No big deal there. We just need to make sure they have a couple of days at the funeral home so they can see their friends when they come to pay their respects, right?" Kathy knows the drill.

Nino agrees. "To be safe, why don't we plan on a Tuesday evening Rosary and a Friday morning funeral Mass? That works best for the priests from the Seminary. I've already checked, and that's what they told me. That will also give people three full days to *view* Mom while she's being laid-out."

Ouch.

"You know how many people loved her," Nino adds. "They're all gonna want to see her."

His words hit me like a dart. I know the last thing Marge wants is for us to have a confrontation over this. I back off to let his words percolate.

Kathy nods. She is in complete agreement.

With no apology for his earlier antics, Nino explains that he came home from the funeral home to make some calls. He says he's already arranged for an uplifting *White Resurrection Mass* for our Mom. "It'll be concelebrated," he tells us.

"That is great, Nino." I thank him for his efforts, even though all I want to do is punch his lights out for deserting me earlier. Of course, I didn't go there, despite the fact that I knew it was going to be impossible for me to sing *Hallelujah* at Marge's funeral. Nonetheless, I gave him his due.

Kathy asks about "*Concelebration.*" It's a fancy term for a High Mass involving more than one priest.

"Mom's Funeral Mass will be said by *three* priests from Sacred Heart Major," Nino explains. "Father Cunningham will take the lead," he tells us, referring to one of the founders of "*Focus Hope,*" an inner city, inter-racial, faith-based initiative created to begin the healing in the aftermath of last summer's devastating riots. The involvement of Father Cunningham would have pleased Marge.

Another thank you to Nino from Kathy follows. She is honored that Marge will have more than one priest say her funeral Mass.

"That's rare treatment for an ordinary citizen of the Church, isn't it, Mikee?"

I nod at Nino. Kathy hugs him for all his efforts.

All the while, Patrick is showing no interest in any of the details. Though still within earshot, he stays in the living room waiting for the President's speech to be over so he can resume watching highlights from some bowling tournament.

I grab Bubba by the jowls and give him a big kiss on the top of his head. It earns a bloodshot gaze. He licks my chin then settles in at my side with one of his patented gangster leans. He rests his head on my lap. The nubs of my knuckles find the under-flaps of his ears. *Ooooooh. Good Boy.*

I dive back in. "Now that we have her Funeral Mass nailed down, let's talk about the funeral home service. Okay?"

"What's there to talk about?" Kathy wonders.

Bubba sighs.

I explain.

"Well, I was talking to Mom a few weeks ago. She asked me to make sure that we have a closed casket for her."

Nino glares. "What?"

"I have already arranged it," I explain. "The funeral home owner is onboard. Everything is set. I just thought you should know."

Nino explodes. "Mom did not! You are making that up! You just want to be in charge and I won't have it. I am the one who is going to be a priest. I'm the one who knows about these things! You are lying, Mikee. It *has* to be an open casket. That's the only way it's done! You are a damn liar."

Poor Kathy doesn't deserve this.

I suck in a breath.

"A closed casket?" she asks without a bit of fuss.

God, I so appreciate her composure.

"Does that mean people won't be able to view the body at the funeral home, like they did for Dad?" she wonders.

"It's unheard of!" Nino screams.

"Hey, hey, pipe down, for Christ's sake. I'm trying to watch some bowling in here." Patrick has become his father.

"It's what Mom wanted," I offer, in support of Kathy's measured tone. "I swear to God. Listen, please. Why would I make this up? Mom and I talked about it at length, and she was very specific. She told me that the casket should only be opened once for a private viewing for Bob and Claire when they arrive from Florida, and for no one else. Those are the instructions I gave the funeral home. That's the way it *has* to be."

"You are lying!" the broken record wails again.

Jesus help us.

Nino is shaking now. "I can't believe you gave those instructions to the funeral home director without consulting me!" So says the young man who had spent two days stonewalling before abandoning me earlier at the funeral home business office.

Kathy is puzzled. Unless the deceased is a disfigured victim of a car accident or a gunshot wound, the casket is always open to allow mourners to approach and gape. Even limo-bound victims of SIDS are subjected to open casket viewings in our neighborhood.

"But what will people think if the casket is closed, Mikee?" Kathy asks. Her composed demeanor is helping.

I stand to speak to anyone willing to listen. "They will remember Mom as she was, Kath. They will remember her as she wants them to; happy and vibrant, filling rooms with her laughter and always ready to lend a hand to those in need. That's what they'll take away."

Nino's tirade continues. "You are full of shit, Mikee."

Bubba shifts. Beefy jowls find Kathy's lap. She massages our big boy's shoulders. "When you put it that way, it sounds wonderful," Kathy agrees. "Let's have a closed casket if that's what Mom told Mikee she wanted."

Bubba looks up with a dreamy gaze when Nino announces that he feels this decision excludes him. "Fine. If it's a closed casket then I am no longer part of this family. It's official."

He promises to do nothing more to help with the service. And he doesn't. Our relationship with Nino changed forever when he exited our lives that day.

TWENTY-NINE

ROAD DUST

Bob and Claire arrive from Florida in a car looking worse for wear. It's covered with bug splatter and road dust.

We greet them with enormous hugs. I show them to our parents' bedroom. While they unpack, Patrick insists we head outside to give their old Mercury a good scrubbing.

"Good thinking, buddy," I praise him.

While Patrick shines the inside of the windshield, empties the ash tray and works some magic on the dusty dash, Bubba lies in a puddle, licking his reflection from a hubcap. I am brandishing a soft cloth on the headlights and hood when our grandfather appears on our front porch. "Moykee, Paddy, come over here, wudja?" He smiles. "The car looks good, boys. Moytee good. Moy Gawd. Look at those wheels, wudja? I've *never* seen 'em shine that way. C'mon in, now. Your grandmother has hot food on the table."

It's ten the next morning. I am back at the funeral home with my grandparents by my side. The staff has rolled Marge to a small empty side room for a private viewing. After brief introductions, the owner puts on white gloves and opens her casket. I turn to leave so Bob and Claire can have some time alone. I have no desire to look.

Thirty minutes later, I return. I saunter toward Claire and give her a tearful hug. Bob joins. We all hold on tight and cry. I steal a peek.

Oh dear Lord, I can't believe it. I forgot Mom's engagement ring and wedding band....

A short while later, the owner hands me a little satin bag containing the rings, which he had retrieved at my request. When I arrive home, I give the little pouch to Kathy. "God, can you believe we almost forgot these, Mikee? Thank you. Thank you. Oh my word. To think that we almost buried Mom with these on."

It's a three-day vigil in front of her casket, where many kind words are spoken. *"If there is ever anything we can do,"* becomes a mantra. We must have heard those words five hundred times. As happens, however, as soon as it was over, most people moved on, forgetting their kind offerings of help.

In the days that follow, Kathy assumes the role of Wendy Darling, the girl from *Peter Pan*. Loving. Supportive. Trusting. Hard working.

Within a week we all get busy. Kathy's schedule allows no time to dwell on matters beyond her control.

Still furious, Nino has returned to the Seminary.

I resume my sophomore year of high school.

Patrick joins a fraternity of Lost Boys.

He's off to NeverLand.

THIRTY

FLYING SOLO

It's as if the memory of Marge cast a spell on our neighbors who all give us space, thank God. Showing respect for Kathy, no one interferes. A short while before, Marge told her twenty-one-year-old daughter she had nothing to fear. *"They're smart boys, honey. You'll be fine. Your brothers have had plenty of time to figure this out. Just let them know you love them. From this point on, it's up to them."* With no papers to sign or court proceedings to attend, Kathy becomes our de facto guardian. Our jobs are clear. Heed Marge's direction:

"Stay under the radar."

Kathy's work hours increase. Week in and week out, she makes sure there is food on the table. And she always makes the mortgage payment on time. All without a whimper. *"Don't sweat the small stuff,"* Marge taught her. Truth is, Kathy doesn't sweat the big stuff either. She rolls with it. *"Just pray that they stay out of jail,"* she remembers Marge telling her with a laugh.

So, every night, Kathy says a simple prayer that her brothers will all behave. Beyond that, she knows there is not a lot she can do. She is not equipped to give us direction, nor is that expected. Nonetheless, there isn't a more loving sister or loyal worker-bee on the planet. On her feet for ten hours a day, often seven days a week, she becomes a fixture as a cashier at our neighborhood grocery. And when the mail arrives on the third of each month, she hands over our $134 Social Security checks to each of us. She has no obligation to do it that way. That's just how she decides to do it.

Nino keeps his distance. It's rare that we see him.

Having just become a teenager, Patrick is preparing to take full advantage of circumstances. He is also growing and packing on weight. Tilting the scales at over 300 pounds, he is a massive *boy-man* who is spending the majority of his time hustling unsuspecting adults in bowling alleys for hundreds of dollars a clip. Following in his father's footsteps, his attendance at school becomes spotty. With no one to hound him, he rather likes being on his own. He gets up when he wants and he goes out when he wants. Blessed with street smarts, a natural aptitude for math and stellar instincts, he shows up at school just often enough to avoid allegations of truancy and to hand out his NFL betting sheets to the seventh grade science teacher who also plays the organ in church.

For my part, I am lucky to be attending Detroit Catholic Central, a competitive all-boys school, run by The Order of Basilian Fathers out of Toronto, home of my longtime *Hockey Night in Canada* heroes. An anonymous benefactor made it possible for me to attend CC, a school rich in history and tradition that included football match-ups against a team from Father Flanagan's Boys Town from Nebraska back in the 1930s.

Between hockey, track, cross-country and a full course load of Algebra II, Biology, French, Civics and AP English, there aren't enough hours in my day for me to get into trouble. Besides, I am obsessed with earning my varsity letter before the end of my sophomore year. Making the Track Team is my last shot at glory.

I have two months to prove myself.

"I really want this, Mom. I really do," I remember telling her a few weeks earlier. Now thinking back, I don't know what I would have done if I wasn't running during Marge's last days. Those workouts were like an elixir to keep me level-headed and focused.

"*Work hard. Listen to your coaches. Be smart. That's all you can do, Mikee. You run; I'll pray,*" she told me that day when she gave me her AA medal.

THIRTY-ONE

THE BOOKIE IN THE FAMILY

It's a Saturday morning, two weeks after Marge's funeral. Hose in hand, I am making my way into the backyard to fill Bubba's bowl, which is something that we all agreed to take turns doing. I do it most often. Splayed on the cool cement, our mighty king of hydration is inside the garage, lying not far from where the baby sparrow fell from its nest years before. The memory of Marge cleaning up that little mess that day brings a smile.

Bubba is making happy breathing sounds. "*HEH-HEH-HEH-HEH.*" Spittles of drool fall from his mouth. Crusty yellow mucus, which Marge calls *haw*, fills the corners of his bloodshot eyes. Bending down to wipe away his sleep with my thumb, I can't resist giving him a big kiss on top of his muzzle. He takes a deep breath as I do and then he offers me a warm nuzzle before resting his chin in the puddle next to his bowl. It's a well-deserved respite for our big boy, who spent the morning running around the yard chasing butterflies near Marge's favorite rosebush.

Patrick is carrying a shovel as he comes around the corner of the garage. It looks like he's been working at the base of the telephone pole in the back corner of our yard. Now he's digging up the small brick surrounds of flowerbeds that frame our garage door. He is strewing dirt all over the driveway, and whistling. It's all terribly odd. Never in his life has he shown the least bit of interest in gardening.

"Hey, buddy, what are you doing?"

He doesn't look up to respond. "Just looking for the cash box, Mike."

"Excuse me, Pat? What are you talking about? What cash box?" I inquire.

"There has never been a bookie in the history of Detroit who hasn't kept a box of cash somewhere, in case of an emergency. I'm looking for Dad's stash. That's all," he states, casual and composed.

"Huh? Pardon me? Dad was a chef, Pat." I say it like he needs to be reminded.

"Oh, right, I forgot. I must be confused. Stupid me." He stares with a smirk. "Mikee, Dad was also a bookie. C'mon, you knew that. Everyone in the city knew Dad took action," says Tony's now thirteen-year-old protégé.

I can't believe what I'm hearing. "Dad worked for the mob? No way!"

"Hey! Watch your mouth. *Ixnay* the *Obmay*." Patrick is dead-serious. "Get something straight, right now. First off, as Dad used to say every time he was asked about the 'M' word, *'There is no such thing as the mafia.'* Got it, Mikee? Secondly, what are you, lame?" he continues. "What do you think Dad did with his free time after cooking lunches for the ad executives? Why do you think he came home so late every night? Don't you remember him hanging out at the Lions' Summer Camp over at Cranbrook? And what do you think golfers do at places like Chandler Park and Rackham? They bet, for Chrissake! When Dad wasn't out there taking action, he was over at Argyle Lanes keeping busy. Do you think those truck drivers for Fisher Meats were just being nice when they backed into our driveway to unload steaks every couple of weeks? Dad was a bookie. Those drivers did his bidding for him. I've known it for years, ever since the night we started wagering at the *Americana* across from Crown. Dad took action from all comers on how many pancakes I could eat. We cleaned up. That was the night we became partners. We made a buck for each one I put down past twenty."

"And?"

"I ate over a hundred…they were just 'silver dollar' size, though," he boasts.

"So, *why* are you digging up the flowerbeds?"

"Mikee, the flowerbeds are the last place left to look for Dad's stash of cash. He died all of a sudden. Now that Mom's gone, I figure I'd better go through every hiding place around the house to find his cash box. I've searched the rafters. I've looked in the fruit closets in the basement. I even broke through the tin surround on our milk chute."

"And?"

"And after all of my searching, I think I figured something out."

"What's that, buddy?" I can't wait to hear this one.

"I think Marge should have been the bookie in the family, Mikee," he says with a smile.

Heading into the house, I bestow a vigorous shoulder-rub-hug just hard enough to make him squeak out a little laugh.

Flowers are blooming in May when I earn my varsity letter. With a 63-split I ran a personal-best 2:09 in the 880 at a track meet at archrival U of D High. I did it! I can't wait to get home to share the news. Then I remember that no one will be there, except of course for Bubba. As soon as I walk through the door, he begins licking my face with a sweet vengeance. *He* knows something big just happened.

Together, we sit. Beneath the kitchen table, I tell him all about the events of my day.

THIRTY-TWO

Though not quite sixteen, I learn that I'm eligible to join my first union. Retail Clerks it is, bagging groceries at Kathy's store, where I had begun working off the clock for cash as a casual laborer back when I was thirteen. A manager named Nobel, hired me each winter to shovel snow. In summer, he paid me to sickle weeds, sweep the parking lot, and keep loose skids orderly in the back of the store.

Now I'm punching-in at 4pm, four days a week. It's a perfect schedule, since it allows me to play baseball in a mid-day City Parks & Rec League over at Stoepel No.2. Occasionally I skate, sometimes at two in the morning, playing hockey with Kathy's night crew at a Westside rink called Winter Wonderland. Dues and withholdings aside, if it wasn't for working under a collective bargaining agreement to earn a fair wage, I could never have afforded those extravagant late night outings with guys from the neighborhood who were old enough to drive. So, life is good. Most mornings, I snooze, except for Thursdays, which I keep free for yard work. Mowing, edging, sweeping, and picking up after our big boy is something Kathy appreciates and with Bubba by my side, it's a task I enjoy.

I'm making my last pass on the front lawn when I hear news reports blaring from a car radio. Bobby Kennedy is dead. I don't want to believe he was shot to death in Los Angeles. Was it just five years ago that Marge told her favorite fifth grader to write a letter to Caroline and little John-John? *"Let them know how you are feeling, Mikee. Put it down on paper. Mail it,"* Marge told me. Now, our lives are being ground to a halt yet again. Dallas. Memphis. Los Angeles.

Two months before, Kathy, Nino, Pat and I were together to watch the news detailing the assassination of Dr. King on the eve of Marge's concelebrated funeral Mass. I tried to comfort myself by imagining them in Heaven together, fast becoming friends. The next day I had it in my heart to stay strong for Kathy. I wanted to emulate young John-John who saluted the coffin when it passed, and be like little Caroline, so steadfast and strong for her mom. So I shed no public tears during Marge's funeral Mass or at the graveside service that followed.

Today is going to be different. Today I'll let it out. Today I'll have my first good cry since I switched that bedside tape to *Pas de Deux*.

As I push the mower back into the garage, Bubba joins in slow lock step. As we sit together on the shady cement, my faithful listener doesn't mind one bit that I'm crying my eyes out as he licks my salty cheeks. I tell him all about Senator Kennedy. I quote his words, which Marge used so often to inspire me. *"The greatest truth must be recognition that in every man, in every child, is the potential for greatness."* Lick…lick. "Wanna hear a story, Bubba?" Lick…lick. "Wanna hear a story?" Ears perk. My big boy sits tall. I tell him about a disappointment I had a few years ago and how Marge chose Senator Bobby's words to comfort me. *"Only those who dare to fail greatly can ever achieve greatly,"* she told me on that day which seems so long ago. Now, all of her heroes are falling. "God save her maestro," I hear myself mutter. First to go was her *"Good Pope John."* Then it was President Kennedy in Dallas. Four years later, it was Dr. King. Now, two months since Memphis, we've lost Bobby in Los Angeles.

Bubba pushes his muzzle under my chin. Snuggle, snuggle, hug, hug. *"HEH-HEH-HEH-HEH."* His demeanor is exemplary.

For the better part of the next hour, together we sit. I cry. I kiss his head. I give him hugs. I wipe away his haw. I thank him for being here for me while I hold on tight.

When it's time to head in, I imagine hearing Marge's words from two years before, when we stood in the alleyway, behind the vet's office. She is giving my arm a loving squeeze. *"It's ok to be sad, Mikee."*

With that, I cry some more.

A glorious summer ensues. Mid-July I get my license. I'm legal to drive at long last. Tiger games blare from every car radio in the city. Twenty-four-year-old Denny McLain is giving new meaning to the term *"juicing"* as reports circulate that he drinks a case of Pepsi a day. He would make 44 appearances during that regular season, pitching a remarkable 336 big league innings. At 31-6 with a 1.96 ERA, he carried our town on his back to the World Series, where everyone's favorite southpaw, Mickey Lolich, became our Fall Classic hero. After a respectable 17-9 regular season, the doughnut-munching Mickster made World Series history with three complete game wins, as the Tigers beat Bob Gibson's Cardinals in seven.

The pendulum had swung.

Good times followed sad when the riot worn *Mudville* of my boyhood celebrated, together as one, up and down Grand River, where my high school buddy Raymond and I slow cruised beneath streams of toilet paper roll tosses, yelling and cheering, as crowds banging pots and pans spilled onto the street. The Tigers became World Series champs for the first time since Tony was courting Marge. We did it! In the wake of the scars left by the riots a year before, every soul in our city felt like we'd earned it.

THIRTY-THREE

MOON LANDING!

It's the summer of WOW.

For America and most of the world, nothing could beat the intensity and excitement of the moon landing in July of '69; unless you're living in the MikeeZone, that is. Neil Armstrong's little stroll outside the LEM paled in comparison to the Sea of Tranquility my girlfriend Natalie and I found, a few weeks before, snuggling on a planet of soft cotton bedding upstairs in our house on Faust.

What's a boy to do?

It began with a stack of my sister's classic 45s on the turntable in her bedroom.

"Walking in the Rain" by the Ronettes drops first. Nattie and I hug and shuffle.

Smokey Robinson's *"Ooh Baby Baby"* follows. That brought us to the edge.

When Barbara Mason sang, *"Yes, I'm ready,"* we lost it altogether.

Best dance of my young life, that was.

Now a few weeks later, Natalie and I are sitting in her living room, watching Walter Cronkite with her brother and widowed mom. A live transmission crackles. *"One...small step...for man..., one...giant leap...for...mankind."* As the stars and stripes are planted in moon dust, Natalie excuses us to the front porch. Standing close, she fidgets with the buttons on the front of my shirt.

"I'm late," she tells me. A tear streams down her cheek.

"Uh, whaddya mean, you're late? Where are you supposed to be, Nattie? I can take you. Let me run home and get the car," I offer. Clueless.

"I'm not supposed to *be* anywhere, Michael. I'm trying to tell you that I...I think we're pregnant."

Huh?

I pull her close.

A few weeks before, we had gone a bit beyond the stage of a passionate kiss in the backseat of a car. That was the day I told my saint of a sister that the love of my young life and I were planning to "spend some alone time together" upstairs in our house. Trusting as ever, Kathy doesn't mind a bit that we'd be spending some time in her bedroom after she leaves for work. After all that we had been through together, I shouldn't have been surprised by Kathy's reaction. "That's fine, Mikee. No worries. Do you want me to pick up a Honeybaked Ham and some skinny-necked Pabst for you guys, for later?"

What a dear. I had never even tasted a beer. No desire to yet.

"Aw, Kath. No. We'll be fine. We're just gonna snuggle a little while you're at work, maybe listen to some records. I have to be at the store myself at four. I just wanted to let you know that your bedroom is where we'll be hanging out."

"No problem. Have fun. See you later. Love you, Mikee. Bye."

Ok then…hit it, lads.

"…*Well, she was just seventeen…and you know what I mean…and the way she looked was way beyond compare….*"

Cha-cha-cha…

Sexy, sweet, loving and smart, Natalie is a year older than I am, so she was ahead of me throughout our years at St. Suzanne. She now attends Rosary, same as Kathy did. Not long after Marge's passing, she invited me to take her to her junior prom. Although I was not *officially* legal to drive at fifteen, Kathy let me take the car on that big date, just as she suspected Marge would have done. After the dance, Natalie and I sat in front of her house talking until two in the morning. We've been together ever since. Alone time with her is like being with a temptress from a James Bond movie. *Oholymoly*. And she loves to read, which makes her even more of a goddess, by my standards.

At long last, a lazy summer afternoon presents itself. Nattie has the day off from her job in the executive offices of the JL Hudson Company downtown on Woodward. The thought of playing baseball that day didn't even enter my mind.

The memory that lingers most is the beautiful blush on her cheeks when I looked into her eyes and held her close, under the guise of an early present for me. She became the girl inside my birthday cake that day. Unhurried, we luxuriated in the warmth of being together. Nothing else in the world existed...except for the radio.

Van Morrison is singing "*...down in the hollow, we are playing a new game....*" Of course I knew better than most that actions have consequences, especially when you're not quite seventeen. I just didn't care to believe that being alone in bed with the most beautiful girl in the world could be life altering.

Whoa, Nelly. Whoa.

Seriously.

We're in the back of an empty aircraft...flying to Paris, perhaps. Fast and furious came the announcement from the pilot. Engines moan. The plane is going down. Our tickets are about to be punched. There's only one thing to do.

We decided to go out big.

We're gliding now...kissing...loving...soaring high over the Atlantic...basking in the glory of feeling our hearts beat as one...oh yeah...

Of course, our plan was never to risk our futures. We were both just looking for an hour or two of soft, sweet, wondrous intimacy, as we disrobed and slipped under the covers to listen to some music and hold each other tight as we hurtled through the air; floating in free-fall, to a destiny beyond our control.

Man. That was sumpthin'.

It's been a week since the moonwalk. With no update for a few days, I am heading over to Natalie's to break the news to her mom. Void of trepidation, I am feeling surprisingly calm, unlike the other walks I have had to take through the neighborhood during my young life. I imagine I'll soon be studying hydrant hook-up configurations for a test that will allow me to become a firefighter. I am ready to step up. I'll do whatever it takes to provide for my family, if that's my destiny. So be it.

Natalie greets me on the front porch. Again she twirls the buttons on my shirt, only this time she looks up with a smile. There's news. It was a false alarm. "I guess it just wasn't our time, Michael," she whispers.

We hug. We laugh. We kiss and hug some more. Hand in hand, we stroll around the block, still smiling. And although I know in my heart that it's not my first mulligan by a long shot, it definitely serves as a wakeup call. Given our tender ages, we both thank our lucky stars to have survived so that we might fly again another day; next time more safely, for sure.

THIRTY-FOUR

HEAVY'S WORLD

Patrick meanwhile is becoming known all over town as *Heavy*. Looking back upon those days, I'm reminded that spending time in his element makes me feel like I am co-starring with Denzel Washington in *Training Day*. Ever the Ethan Hawke rookie, I struggle to match wits with his *Alonzo*, especially when I join him to bowl a few frames. After handing over a weeks' pay that I had earned the summer before, I earn an admonishment as he pockets my money. "Consider that a lesson. The hustle is not a dance, Mikee. When you're hustling you are making your mark do something they would never do in a million years. And when you're good at it, you come to know the best part of all. The mark doesn't even know when it's happening," he boasts.

A natural "righty," Heavy bowls lefty until he can entice a mark to raise the ante of a *friendly* wager. He also knows how to load-up a bowling ball, whatever that means, although he swears he only does so for an occasional tournament, "to even the odds when the lanes are oily."

I'm clueless. *Huh?*

Scoping the scene, he identifies a balding man with a bulge of bills in his pocket. Patrick spotted him earlier buying a round at the bar, flaunting a wad of cash. "A *nickel a pin,*" is Heavy's proposition. It sounds innocent until Heavy announces with great dismay that he can't believe he is "down a grand" after just ten frames. Incredulous, the mark wonders how he could be up by so much. "Wasn't that for a *nickel* a pin?" the older man asks.

Heavy feigns surprise. He makes it clear that "a nickel" means fifty bucks, of course. He congratulates his mark profusely before wagering one more game at double the amount he is down. Switching to righty, Heavy nets ten nifty C-Notes for about an hour's work.

Following the example of his grandfather, thoroughbred racing also becomes one of his all-consuming passions. The DRC, otherwise known as The Detroit Race Course, becomes one more home away from home for Heavy. Depending on his success reaching out to jockeys or trainers whom he rewards for information, Heavy is up and down, but mostly up. Knowing the ropes as he does, he also knows when to lay low by scheduling occasional road trips.

He is with his buddies, coming home from a successful outing at a track called Woodbine near Toronto. In the trunk of their car is a duffle stuffed with $32,000 in Canadian bills. There's also an array of contraband and some easy to recognize paraphernalia, compliments of his thirty-something colleagues. The bag also holds hundreds of losing ticket stubs, which they collect religiously upon the advice of associates who represent themselves as authorities on taxes.

Nearing the checkpoint on the Detroit side of the Windsor Tunnel, pink-cheeked Heavy volunteers to take the lead.

"Welcome to the United States, gentlemen. Citizenship and place of birth, please."

From habit, they reply one at a time. "United States, sir. Detroit, sir."

"How long have you been out of the country, gentlemen?"

"Less than a day, sir," Patrick offers.

"Do you have any fireworks in this vehicle, young man?"

"No sir, no fireworks, sir," he responds.

"How about firearms…are you carrying any firearms in this vehicle?"

"No, sir. No firearms in this vehicle, sir," Heavy swears.

"Do any of you have more than $10,000 in currency in your possession?"

"Absolutely not," says Heavy without hesitation, hoping that would put an end to the matter and allow them to proceed on home.

"Ok, boys. In that case, why don't you pop the trunk? We'll take a quick look inside," the official demands.

Heavy glances at the ID pinned to his shirt.

"Hey, are you aware that you have three sevens in your badge number? Sevens are lucky, you know," Patrick offers.

"Just pull over there, pop the trunk and settle down, buddy."

"Seriously. Do you mind if I ask you a question?" Heavy presses. "If I had a badge number like that, I would have to believe I was lucky. So tell me, since you're a lucky guy. If you had a choice, would you rather be famous or would you rather be rich?" As he poses the question, Heavy reaches into his breast pocket and pulls out ten colorful Canadian hundreds. Fanning the bills on his chest, he makes sure the border guard is focused on him. Then, in full view, he calmly folds the currency to match the size of his palm. Looking the customs official straight in the eye, he offers a final query, "Sorry, sir. I don't think I heard you. Did you say famous, or did you say rich?" Heavy pushes.

They are back home in Grosse Pointe Park ten minutes later.

On Wednesday evenings traffic is light.

Before Patrick moves out to live on his own, shiny cars, black like crows, appear all too often in our driveway. While I ride the bus during my junior year of high school, Lincoln Continentals with suicide doors become young Patrick's mode of transportation. Day in and day out, he rumbles down the stairs as his ride idles in the driveway.

"Heading to the track, Pat?" I ask him.

"Not today…just goin' fishin' with Jimmy Q and a few of the guys. They have a boat out on some deep-water lake."

Patrick is alone when I get back from my cross-country practice. He's sitting in the living room, watching TV in the dark.

"So, how was fishing? Were they biting?" I pester.

"No, they weren't biting so good," he replies flatly.

"Whaddya mean? Didn't you catch anything, Pat?"

"Whaddya mean…Didn't you catch anything???" He mocks. It sounds like he's been drinking. "Are you talkin' to me, Mikee? Do you really want to know whassup?"

He's off the couch. We're standing toe-to-toe.

I can't resist. "Yeah, I really want to know, Pat. How was fishing?" I hold his stare. We're nose-to-nose now. I am not about to flinch, especially if my little brother has come home with a goose egg for his efforts out on some lake this afternoon. It is, after all, just playful razzing.

"Fishin' wasn't so good because the guys I went out with - they were pros but they weren't professional anglers," he answers.

Obnoxious, I push. "So what's the problem…you didn't catch any fish, didja Pat? Is that it?"

"Mikee, fishin' wasn't so good because my friend, Jimmy Q…he didn't make it back off the lake."

His words hung in the air as he stared into my soul. I didn't know what to believe. He offered no details and I didn't pursue it. I later told myself he fabricated that story, just to keep me guessing; as if I needed convincing that my little brother's life was becoming a cluster. Whatever his intent, it worked. I never again asked him where he was going or what he was doing.

Best we go separate ways, I figured.

I have no time for distractions anyway, especially since hockey practices take me to the far side of the border a few times a week. To save on expenses, CC Varsity works out at a municipal rink in Riverside, Ontario, where two hours of practice is a quarter of the cost of an hour of ice time in Detroit. Our coach, a priest we call *Punch*, drives our white school bus to and from Canada, always in heavy traffic, always through the tunnel. On those nights, I'm lucky if I get home by nine.

It's a typical Tuesday night. It is almost ten o'clock and I've just walked through the door. I have homework to do. And I need to be back at school no later than 7:30 tomorrow morning. Kathy enters the kitchen, insisting on making me a bite to eat. God love her. Stretched out under the table, my furry footrest awaits. Placing my practice-worn feet on his belly, I rub. Bubba sighs like he might be dreaming about Marge. Kathy has just arrived home from work herself. She is as devoted to her store as she is to her brothers. I'm too exhausted for anything but small talk. I ask her how she's doing.

"Oh, I'm glad you asked, Mikee. Today did not go well. The store got robbed."

"Huh? Our store, right here in the neighborhood? Robbed? Tell me what happened, Kath."

"A guy came up to the manager's office wearing a mask. He had collected everyone's purses and wallets and emptied them into the frozen food cases; you know, the ones that are barely waist-high. It made it easier for his little cohort to pick through everything for money and valuables. Then the guy with the gun held it to my head and told me to open the safe."

"Oh my God, Kathy. Are you ok?"

I move to hug her. She keeps me at arm's length.

"I'm fine, Mikee, really. I just told him I didn't have the combination so he went back to the frozen food bin, signaled the other guy and they ran out. All they got were the contents of some purses, a few wallets and some watches."

"Wow, how lucky was that, Kath! Thank God you didn't know the combo."

"Mikee, I'm the Assistant Head Cashier. Of course, I know the combination. I just didn't want the bad guys to get our store's money."

Apparently Marge forgot to tell her what she had repeatedly told me since back when I was a little one, heading out by myself past the high school to get a haircut. *Always give up the damn money, Mikee. It's not worth it. Just toss it one way and run the other.*

THIRTY-FIVE

AN AFTERNOON AT THE DIA

Bubba now champions life at home. Between Kathy's work schedule, Patrick's nefarious adventures and Nino's long-standing absence, our magnificent beast has become our gatekeeper-in-chief. Even during these tumultuous times, his presence makes us feel like we're still a family. Sort of.

Neighbors have begun voicing quiet concern. Can't blame them, really. With Tony and Marge dead and gone, our household is being led by a dog the size of a small horse and a young girl who is informally acting as guardian for her now seventeen and fifteen-year-old brothers. Motivated by whispers, I become dedicated to yard work. Thanks to Bubba's presence, keeping up the lawn feels like happy-time therapy.

My days all run together.

Arriving home late one Wednesday, I find a message on a notepad by the phone. *"Mrs. Church called. You need to meet her — Thursday at noon."*

Marge's best friend bears a striking resemblance to the woman who would become our first female Secretary of State, Madeleine Albright, with whom she would also come to share world-view sensibilities. Her infectious Hungarian spirit makes it impossible to say anything but *"where and when"* when Mrs. Church extends an invitation for a get-together, especially when her venue of choice is the Detroit Institute of Arts.

We meet with a big hug inside the Farnsworth Entrance.

"God, it's good to see you, Mrs. Church. Don't you look wonderful? How's your day going?" I ask, not expecting an answer.

Her hair is in a tight bun on top of her head. She is wearing a flowing black muumuu. It's accented by a turquoise and gold necklace, with earrings and shiny gold sandals to match. She looks like she just stepped out of a travel brochure. "Oh my. What a day. It could not be better, Michael. Thanks for asking. I woke up early, as usual. After my yoga, I stood on my head for ten minutes, which I love. You know that I do that, right? While my tea steeps? Well, this morning was absolutely fabulous. A little yoga, twenty minutes of transcendental meditation, a hot cup of tea. Perfect way to start the day."

I had no idea.

"Listen, there's something I've been meaning to tell you, dear heart. How long has it been since Marge passed, honey?"

"Gosh, it's hard to believe, it's been a year, Mrs. Church."

"Well, what I need to tell you is that your mom has left you a little gift. It's me! Let's make sure you and I keep in touch so we can share your successes together, you, me and Marge, okay?"

"Okay."

"She's still with us, you know, Michael, and we are so proud of you. Tell me, how is school going? You're at CC, right?"

Over coffee in Kresge Court, I'm remembering how refined and civilized Marge would make me feel whenever we talked about her books or current events. Moments later, we are surrounded by Diego Rivera's magnificent *Detroit Industry* murals. They depict sequences of assembly-line workers at the Rouge Plant. I can't hide my smile when I look to see if my grandfather might be memorialized somewhere on those walls.

Mrs. Church engages. "Listen. All that your mom planned and hoped for you is within your reach. Just keep me apprised of your plans. Won't you? That's really all I wanted to discuss with you. Ok?"

A tour of the museum follows. There are paintings by Pablo Picasso, Paul Cezanne, Morris Louis, Henri Matisse, Vincent van Gogh, and Clyfford Still. After I learn about the virtues of *negative space*, our afternoon ends at The Traffic Jam, on Second and Canfield, with a sandwich piled high with hot ham and swiss on warm pumpernickel. Throughout our lunch, Mrs. Church continues to talk about artists and their works as if they are old friends. We chat about theater and literature, and the war, and about current events, just as Marge and I would have.

THIRTY-SIX

THE PLAN

Taking it one day at a time, my future remains fluid. At least I have a plan. I will finish high school. That much is certain, thanks to my benefactor who is continuing to pay my high school tuition. Maybe I'll become a firefighter, after all. Who knows? I hold a glimmer of hope about attending college, but if past experience is any guide, I can't be sure of anything. I just hope I can avoid going off to fight in a war that has no clear objectives. Too many of Patrick's buddies had to go that route after being drafted. Most returned with the predictable emotional baggage. Some came home with bricks of *China White*.

"It's all good, Mikee. Don't worry about me," Patrick assures. "They're just chippers. They snort, is all. Joey Mattucci did it every day in Nam and he's still not hooked."

Aw, Heavy, Heavy, Heavy.

Four-thirty, Thursday afternoon. It's late summer following my junior year. Eddie O'Malley is calling to invite me to meet him at his brother's baseball game. George is pitching right across the street.

A classmate of Nino's throughout all eight years at St. Suzanne, Eddie is the boy who gained notoriety drawing pictures of new model cars on paper plates. His family lives on a street called Minock, down the street from our Catholic Church, in a house the size of a cracker box. Like Natalie's dad, Ed's father was also a cop who passed away when we were kids. It left Ed's mom Tillie on her own to raise a brood of five boys in a house so tiny that Eddie and his brothers didn't have to get out of their seats at the kitchen table during dinner if their mom needed something from one of the cupboards. All they had to do was reach.

"Mikee? Ed here. How are you doing?"

"I'm good, Ed."

"Hey, Nino called. Is he there?"

"Nope. I haven't seen him in over a month, actually."

"That's fine. No big deal. He was trying to track me down. It had something to do with some paper he's working on. Leave him a message by the phone, would ya?"

"You bet."

"Hey Mikee, what grade are you in?"

"I'll be a senior next year."

"So, what are you doing right now? George has a game at five. He'll be on the diamond in front of your house. Why don't you meet me over there? We'll catch up. I want to float something by you."

Twenty paces later, I'm behind the backstop. As usual, there is a healthy crowd of parents and girlfriends milling about since George O'Malley is on the mound working it.

Ed begins, "So, how is CC treating you? How is school going?"

"Everything is going well. Thanks for asking. I'm playing varsity hockey. I'm a co-captain this year. In a few weeks I'll be running cross-country. I'll do track again in the spring. Man, I thank God I'm running, Ed. It keeps me sane."

"So, how's your GPA? How are you doing academically, Mikee?"

"I'm doing ok. Almost a 4.0, but not quite. Why do you ask?"

"Have you taken your Boards, the SATs yet? How did you do on those?" he pushes.

"Yeah, I took 'em. My guidance counselor thinks I might have a shot at Michigan State, actually. Getting in could be my ticket to a 2-S. I'm just hoping for the best."

"Where *are* you applying to college anyway, Mikee?"

"Oh, jeez, Ed. To be honest, I'm not sure I'm gonna do that. You know my situation. Maybe I'll get lucky with the draft lottery so I can become a fireman or somethin'."

Unconvinced, Ed continues. "Don't be ridiculous. You need go to college. In fact, I think you should apply to where I go. You'd love it there. It's terrific."

"Don't you go to *Harvard*, Ed?"

"Yeah, that's right. I'll be a junior next year. Boy, I gotta tell ya, it is one terrific place, and I think Cambridge and Boston would be perfect for you. Look. With your grades, reasonable board scores, and proven self-direction, you might have a real shot at getting in. I mean it, Mikee. No foolin'."

Huh? Gimme a break. He cannot be serious.

"Let me do a little legwork here," he insists. "I think I'll invite the Harvard interviewer over to the house. You guys should meet. Tillie will be happy to make dinner. How does that sound?"

"Gosh, I don't know. I'd hate to waste the guy's time. I *would* like seeing your mom, though. But really, Ed, it sounds way out of my league. Thanks for the offer anyway."

"Come on, Mikee. I bet you'll like him, this interviewer guy *Hocevar.* We call him *Hoc* for short. His first name's Don. Let me take care of the details. All you have to do is show up. How hard is that? Of all people, Mikee, what have *you* got to lose?"

He had a point.

"Ok. You set it up. Just let me know when. I'll be there."

Hocevar tells me that no one from my high school has ever been accepted to attend Harvard — except for one — and that was a decade ago. "So, clearly, you are a long shot."

Tell me something I don't know, why don't ya?

After our meal, we adjourn to the living room. We talk. We thank Tillie for a wonderful dinner. Don suggests we wrap up at a nearby coffee shop. We chat for two more hours.

He calls a week later. All business, he doesn't even say hello when I answer. "Put that application in the mail immediately. Send it to Harvard University, Admissions Office, Holyoke Center, Cambridge, Massachusetts 02138. Do it this week." Click.

It's all so confusing.

The last thing I need is another disappointment in my life.

At this stage, I long for any success. A high number in the draft lottery? Passing the test to become a City Firefighter? Those would do me fine. This Harvard thing has come about way too fast. I feel like I'm being set up, so I hide the application in my bureau.

How could *I* possibly measure up?

Our cross-country team did well at States and my hockey team is rockin'. So I've got that going for me. Thanksgiving brings another call from Ed to confirm that I filled out the application.

I always knew that if I was going to apply at all, I would apply late. In need of a built-in excuse to ease the sting of inevitable rejection, I wait until the first week of January to drop it in the mail. The deadline to apply has long since passed.

It's late March of my senior year. The second anniversary of Marge's passing is fast approaching. I find a message next to the phone; the interviewer guy called. I need to be at his house on Sunday to watch a Red Wings-Bruins game. Perfect. I figure there'll be a crowd of applicants there for a *last hurrah*, prior to the Admissions Committee's letters being sent out in mid-April. They're a good bunch and I'm looking forward to seeing them all. One last time.

Other than *Hoc*, which rhymes with *boast*, I am surprised it's just the two of us in his living room watching the game. It's not the worst scenario. At least he's going to let me down easy when he tells me I'm toast.

At the end of the first period, Hoc ambles into his study. He returns with a porcelain beer stein. It's emblazoned with a seal. The word "VERITAS" is scripted in gold. Inside a crest is the word "HARVARD."

"Here, Michael. This is yours."

"Gee…thanks, Don. That is very nice. I'll keep it on my bookshelf. I appreciate it. Very much. It's a great memento of getting to know you. Thanks for everything, man." I mean it.

He stares.

"Memento? Did you say memento? Only people who *go* to Harvard get mugs like this, Michael."

"I'm honored, Don. I really am. It's a great mug. I appreciate it. You are very kind."

The second period begins. Hoc bounds from his chair, snaps the television off. He paces. "Look. I gave you that mug because I just got early word from the Admissions Committee about your application. The letters won't go out until April 15, but I know the action they are taking on yours."

"That's great, Don. So what's the verdict?" I smile, thinking I know what he is about to tell me.

"They said you have been accepted to Harvard University, young man. It was unanimous, which is quite rare. You're in!" he screams. "This is great news for us."

Huh?

"Don, are you telling me that I've been accepted to *Harvard*? Me? Harvard?"

"That's right, young man. You're going to Harvard!" Big smile. Arms waving.

"Wow. Don, that's great news. Let me go home and talk to my sister about it. I'll get back to you."

"Excuse me? Did you say that you would get back to me? Do you have any idea how difficult it is to get into *an Ivy*, let alone Harvard—and you are telling me that *you* will get back to *me*?"

"That's the way it is, Don. I need to go home and talk to my sister, Kathy, and find out what she thinks."

"Okay. Okay. You're right. Go talk to your sister. Call me tomorrow, would you?"

"You bet, Don. I'll give you a call tomorrow afternoon. By the way, thanks for all of your effort on this. I appreciate it."

I take the mug and shake his hand. Twenty minutes later, I am in our driveway. There's a light on, which means Kathy must be home. She is probably on break. She comes down the stairs buttoning her cashier's smock. I tell her I have news.

"What's up? Be quick. I gotta get going here. I'm on break."

"Kathy, do you remember all the time I spent putting that college application together a couple of months ago? Well, I just got word that I got in to the only school where I applied. I've been accepted to attend Harvard, Kath. It's in Boston. What do you think?"

She looks at me like I just told her the weather forecast calls for clearing skies. "Oh, that's nice. Your mother would be proud of you, Michael, with your being accepted to college and all." Halfway out the door she adds, "I'll leave it up to you to figure out the details and how you're going to pay for this education of yours. I've got to go back to work now. Love you."

She is off.

"I love you too, Kath," I yell at the door that has already closed.

A month later, I'm preparing for my graduation ceremony at Ford Auditorium when news reports confirm twelve students have been shot. There are four dead in Ohio. God. I hate this war and I hate what it's doing to our country. I'm certain that the families of the National Guard, as well as the families of those saints from Kent State would agree.

Allison Krause.

William Schroeder.

Jeffrey Miller.

Sandra Scheuer.

God bless you. God rest your souls. God love your families.

My senior promise was that I would remember their names forever.

THIRTY-SEVEN

BACK FROM BOSTON

Back home after my first year in Cambridge, with a full helping of Aeschylus, Sophocles, Euripides, Aristophanes and Homer behind me, the morning musings of Professor John Finley in Sanders Theatre feel like a dream. The old neighborhood doesn't quite look the same, either. I'm a Teamster this summer. I'm loading the bellies of UPS tandems that are heading from Livonia to a hub back east in Secaucus. It's a lot of long hours and good pay, but it sure isn't something I would want to do for a living. Packages arrive on a conveyor that never stops. Build a wall. Lift-toss, lift-toss, lift-toss. Build another wall. Lift, lift, lift...toss, toss, and toss. The pace is maddening.

Patrick's long gone. He's moved in with a handful of usual suspects on the East Side. Although they physically survived the war, they are all still paying a price, as is Pat, who hit the skids as well. After an eviction, he took refuge in an area called *The Cass Corridor*, where he earned his PHD in survival. God love him. To his unbelievable credit, he sought treatment before briefly carving out an occupation for himself as a drug and alcohol rehab counselor. Now, with those days behind him, he is resuming his career in the "sports entertainment industry." Clean and sober, Heavy is back in action. God love him.

"Your brother is an incredibly sharp guy. He really knows how to run a book," one of his colleagues tells me. "Do you have any idea how hard it is to book baseball? He is really sumpthin'. No foolin', Mikee," his friend spouts proudly.

I haven't a clue.

All I can remember is a story he once told me about one of my little brother's clients who owned a restaurant and who placed wagers every night. Here's how it went down.

"Heavy, you got NBA action?"

"Of course, Mr. Woo. I'm loaded. I have plenty of NBA tonight," he engages.

Each night, that owner placed hefty bets on every NBA game on the schedule. Each morning, Mr. Woo would tally his losses. For each and every game. He never won one. Afterwards, Heavy explained that this went on for fourteen consecutive days. Delighted to take his action, on day fifteen, during the NBA All-Star break, the client called again, right on schedule. "Heavy, you got any NBA tonight?"

"No NBA tonight, Mr. Woo, but I've got some NHL," Heavy told him, which caused his client to scream, "What do you take me for, an idiot? I don't know anything about hockey!"

Such is the life of Heavy, the proud baby boy of a chef who hustled book. Now Patrick is offering his own "pick recommendations" by promoting a *"100% guaranteed win"* on Monday Night Football games.

"How can you promise to guarantee the winner?" I wonder.

Patrick is wondering how I got into college in the first place, let alone Harvard.

"Pay attention, Mr. Ivy Leaguer. My market consists of football junkies all over these great United States of America. There are only two teams playing Monday nights, correct? I split the country down the middle, right along the Mississippi. Half gets my *'team A pick,'* and the other half gets my *'team B pick.'* Depending on the spread, which I pad, regardless of which team comes out on top, I'm a genius in half the country. Get it, Mr. Smarty-pants?"

THIRTY-EIGHT

MARY'S FUNERAL

It's summertime when our grandmother Mary, Tony's mom, passes away. I accompany Kathy to the funeral in the town of Jackson, an hour or so west of Detroit. During the drive, Kathy reminisces.

"Mikee, do you remember when our grandmother would send each of us a card on our birthdays every year?" she asks.

"She never once forgot," I add.

"How about the money inside? Do you remember there was always money inside?"

That, I didn't.

For that matter, neither did Kathy. Marge had told her that one of our dad's sisters would open the envelopes and take the money out before mailing them.

"Pretty cruel, Kath, but I'm not surprised. At least Granma remembered our birthdays, right? She was a good woman. God rest her soul," I tell her.

Arriving at church, the usher insists we sit in the first row pew since we were the only mourners with the same last name as our grandmother. It made sense since all four of our dad's sisters were married and our grandfather had died years ago.

The eulogy begins. The pastor asks everyone to acknowledge the stained glass windows in the church, and to take note of the beautiful carved doors. "We have all of this because of Mary," he announces to the congregation. Then he sizes up two of Tony's sisters with a formidable stare. "Mary died with a rosary in her hand, not a five dollar bill."

The two aunts who had ransacked our house three years before finally got their comeuppance, in public, no less, just as Marge said they would.

"Believe me, their scurrilous behavior will be found out, Mikee. All we can do is pray for them."

I can't keep from turning around to see their faces. Candles are flickering in the back of the Church as my two greedy aunts sink from view. That was the moment when they ceased to exist in my mind. I would never see them again.

We enjoy the drive home.

"Do you have any idea how proud your mother would be of you, attending Harvard and all, Michael?" Kathy says.

"Hey, hey. Let's hold the praise until you attend my graduation in a couple of years, shall we?"

"Hah. Very funny, Mikee."

"Seriously, Kath. You never know."

"I'm coming to see you in Boston whether you graduate or not," she insists with a laugh. "Do you remember what Mom said when President Kennedy got elected? *'I don't care how much fame and fortune his family has; to be Irish and Catholic and to attend Harvard…and to graduate? Wow. Now that's an achievement.'* Mikee, she'd be as proud of you now as she was for him then."

I am remembering a magnificent fifth grade Friday. It's the year before Marge learned of her illness. "After I served an early morning Mass, which Marge attended, she insisted on taking me out for an elegant celebratory breakfast. What we were celebrating, I can't quite recall.

"Sounds like Mom was on a mission, huh, Mikee?"

"Oh my God, Kath. You have no idea. She even let me take the day off from school."

Mirrors with beveled edges cover rich oak panel walls. White linen drapes each table. They serve coffee in cups with saucers, all made of fine china, I noticed, as we were shown to our seats.

Marge begins. "Ok. Pay attention here, Mister. I have a feeling that what I am about to teach you is going to come in handy someday."

We enjoy shirred eggs on top of toasted dark rye, crust removed. There are Lyonnais potatoes, sprinkled with bacon crumbles and *fresh* parsley. Small side-plates hold shallow melon halves filled with berries. The silver service has the markings of something from a previous century. And as much coffee as Marge enjoyed that morning, her cup never once became empty, nor did my water glass, as she schooled me on matters of dining etiquette. She talked about bread knives and butter plates and which fork to use when. I learned that you should ladle a soupspoon *away* when you enjoy a bowl of soup or chowder in a formal setting. I learned that, without exception, a proper young man should *always* rise from his seat when a lady excuses herself from the table and rise again upon her return. She also told me, should I find myself in a situation in which I was unsure, I should wait until someone I trusted took the lead. "You can't go wrong doing that, Mikee. Just remember, be patient."

"Got it, Mom."

"Hey, did I ever tell you that I used to work as a waitress down at the Belcrest, with your dad?"

Of course, I'd heard that a thousand times before.

Her face lights up. "Do me a favor, would ya? Start gathering some cups and saucers, buddy. Bring 'em right over here to our table."

Six trips around the room follow.

"Check this out, Mikee."

Hazel eyes beaming, she rises. Carrying cups and saucers stacked to the ceiling, she prances along the entire length of that dining room. Every time she spots her reflection in a mirror, she lets out a hearty laugh.

I pray the manager is on break. I can't imagine what it would cost if even one of those fine china cups came crashing to the floor.

Marge is still bubbling during our bus ride home. "So what do you think of me? Aren't I something?"

I giggle so hard I give myself the hiccups.

Still driving home from our grandmother's funeral, story begets story. Kathy reminds me of Marge's favorite no-frills Jewish Delicatessen at a mall called Northland. "I'll never forget how smitten that man at the bagel counter was with your mom, Mikee," she reminisces. "He let out the same cry every time Marge walked through the door. *TOASTED ONION...DRY...SHMEAR...TOMATO SIDE...BLACK COFFEE.*"

I remembered. "*Thank you, Sam,*" Marge would charm.

Her favorite deli was located near an outdoor plaza that was home to seasonal exhibits like a tree at Christmas or a plywood bunny at Easter, that sort of thing. I recall standing there with Marge ten years before, inspecting a glass-sided bubble of a structure about half the size of a Silver Stream travel-trailer, so popular in the Sixties. Inside the bubble, a mom, a dad and two kids look to be trapped in an oversized ant farm. They are crawling all over each other, reaching for pre-packaged food to eat. Apparently, they were in their second day of a weekend competition, within full view of passersby at the mall. If they could endure an entire seventy-two hours without killing each other, they would become eligible to win a nuclear fallout shelter of their very own.

Marge can't watch, so we walk.

I'm mystified.

I ask about our neighbors, whose fallout shelter sits right over our fence. "Mom, will we join the Wilsons, next door, if there is a nuclear war?"

She slows her pace to take a seat on the edge of an elevated landscape planter. "Look at these marigolds, still colorful, even in the fall. Aren't they beautiful, Mikee?"

"What will *we* do to stay safe, Mom, when nuclear war comes?" I have to know. "Will *we* be going to a fallout shelter, Mom? Where will *we* go to stay safe?"

Marge doesn't miss a beat. "No, Mikee, we'll just be together as a family. As long as we stay together, we will all be fine."

That ends the matter. A confident answer and a bit of eye contact from my mom make all my fears go away. I never again worried about nuclear war, knowing that staying together would keep us safe.

It's been a few weeks since our grandmother's funeral. I'm back in Cambridge where I've accepted a work-study position as the office assistant at Harvard's Kennedy Institute of Politics. It's after work on a Tuesday evening. I'm sipping a bottle of Bud with an IOP teaching fellow, a brilliant guy who has become my friend and a valuable mentor. We're in a downstairs booth at Charlie's Kitchen. With the drive from Jackson still fresh in my mind, I share the story about Marge's measured reaction ten years prior regarding my concerns about nuclear war. After hearing my little story, my friend Jim responds. He tells me about a similar conversation he had when his young son confronted him on the subject of death and dying four years earlier.

It was the day after Senator Bobby Kennedy's assassination. My friend Jim had been on the road with him for a solid month of days and nights, advancing his Presidential Primary campaign. When Jim finally returned home from California at the end of the first week of June, 1968, his son greeted him with the biggest hug ever.

"Dad, is it true Senator Kennedy was shot?"

"Yes, son, Senator Kennedy was shot."

"Did he die, dad?"

"Yes. Senator Kennedy died."

"Dad, what happens to you when you die?"

My friend Jim tells me that he held his little boy close. "When you die, God places you on top of a beautiful cloud. The sun shines on you all day, and all of your dreams come true."

After a burg

er and another beer, I find myself trying to picture Marge in exactly that way, to no avail.

THIRTY-NINE

IT'S TIME

Summer in the city. The heat is oppressive. My hair is too long. The scruff on my face has me looking like I was born to wear baggy Bermuda shorts and tattered sneakers, and an old Toronto Hockey School jersey that I boosted from a teammate a few years before. I'm wandering the backyard, mindlessly picking up after Bubba. A holler from a neighbor two doors down makes me laugh. "They let you look like that at Princeton?"

"Indeed they do, Mr. Zimmerman. They do indeed." I smile.

No need to correct him.

After a few final passes with the mower, Bubba and I take a break. We set off on a stroll. Edging and sweeping can wait. Before reaching the corner, I'm greeted again from a bit farther down. "Hey, long time, no see, Mikee."

It's one of my best grade school buddies' older brother, who has since become a close friend of Patrick's.

"So what are you up to these days?" he asks.

"Just mowing lawns, Shawn. How about you? What've you been up to?"

"I'm on the vile green liquid program, man. I'm doing better, though."

I am fairly certain he's not referring to Nyquil. *Dear God in Heaven.* I thought I looked bad after a morning of sweaty yard work. Ol' Shawn here has definitely seen better days. At least his dog Fred is still carrying on like a champion. Of all the dogs in the neighborhood, Fred was Marge's favorite by far.

"Maintenance program. Methadone, Mikee," he clarifies, before betting me that it's hot enough to fry an egg on the sidewalk.

This can't be good. Given his hard-edged appearance, I face an imperative to create a diversion. *Confuse him, Mikee.* Anything to keep him from knocking on doors to scavenge for an egg. God forbid. It could mean a coronary for some unsuspecting neighbor.

"How hot do you think it is, anyway?" I ask.

"Geez, it's gotta be a hundred in the shade."

"Hmm. Imagine that. It's winter today in Australia, man," I tell him.

Confuse him I did. Shawn suddenly looks as blank as a chalkboard on the last day of school. Staring at his shoes, he whispers like he's sharing a tip about a horse race, "How the hell did they screw that up, Mikee? Honest to God. How'd they screw that up?"

Mission accomplished.

Prancing proud, Bubba puts on a show for Fred as we hustle away without incident. Back on the driveway, I fill our big boy's water bowl and set it inside the garage so Mr. Magnificent can lie down in the shade.

Mindless yard work never felt so good.

There is something I have been holding back from Kathy. I've been waiting for the perfect moment to present it. But that never came. I am not at all sure how she is going to react. I only know I have to say it.

"We need to sell the house, Kath. I think it's time. It isn't exactly improving with age, and if only for reasons of your safety, I think you should simplify matters. You deserve a nice apartment, maybe somewhere out in the suburbs. Think about that for me, would you? With your seniority in the union, I bet they'd set you up with a job at a new store. After we pay off the mortgage, it might even leave a couple thousand dollars in your pocket."

"Do you really think someone would buy it, Mikee? *Our* house?"

"I think so, Kath. Let me work on that."

After all she's been through and everything she has put up with, I want nothing more than to put a little money in her pocket so she can get on with her life. There is only one problem.

Realizing that there is no way I can pull this off by myself, I enlist the help of one of my best buds, a Harvard roommate, whose family lives in nearby Dearborn. Bob responds without hesitation. "Anything for Kathy," he tells me. Even his dad Joe agrees to pitch in by making a third-party inspection.

Lucky boy, Mikee.

Joe looks just like Broderick Crawford from the 1950s TV program, "Highway Patrol." A gem with a hard crust exterior, he's a pro at everything he sets his mind to, and as tough on himself as he is on his son Bob. Joe makes me laugh like no other parent I know. A magnificent provider for his two boys and his adoring wife Rosie, a bigger sweetheart of a blowhard does not exist.

I greet them at the front door and offer coffee. Joe admits he's had too much already. "Let's just get to it. Time's-a-wastin'. Bob, go to the car. Grab my tools."

I try to find words to thank him. Joe reads me perfectly. As soon as Bob is out of earshot, he gives me a broad smile and shoots me a wink. "Happy to help," he says with his meat hooks on my shoulders. I realize just how much those words mean when Bob returns from the car. Joe suddenly has his game face on when he places blame for forgetting his tape measure. "Damn it, Bob."

"Joe, relax. I think I can find one. Gimme a minute," I assure him.

Bob is undaunted. Despite the demeanor, he knows that his dad is as happy as a mud-covered pig that we asked him to set aside his entire Saturday morning to inspect my childhood home. "We just need to give him a minute. Trust me. He'll warm to it," Bob tells me, knowing that his dad is happiest when he can grumble.

Joe wasn't kidding about the coffee, either. No doubt about it. He'd had plenty already. That was made clear by the pace of his dispatch as soon as I handed him the tape measure.

"Ok, you two. Keep your damn distance. Just stay the hell outta my way. Don't worry. I'll yell if I need ya."

We laugh.

Joe proceeds to open and close each door to inspect where the house may have settled. He checks all of the faucets. He fills the bathtub and each sink to spot issues of blockage. He examines every appliance in the kitchen. He even checks out the furnace in the basement. Outside, he scrapes paint from trim and pounds on the face-brick to ensure the exterior has some years left.

I'm hovering within earshot, hoping for the best.

"Alright. It could be worse, Frick!"

A nickname that stuck thanks to my freshman roommate, Johnny G, only my best friends at Harvard call me *Frick*. I like that Joe does the same.

Standing tall on the driveway, Bubba towers over the gate to the backyard. He's gazing at Joe like he might be hiding a slab of sirloin in his pocket.

Joe is staring at the driveway. As he rubs his chin, our mighty big boy wants nothing more than to crawl over the fence to give Joe a full frontal tongue-lashing to show his appreciation. Bubba knows Joe's opinion is crucial. This is, after all, my childhood home.

As we approach, Joe walks over to give our Mr. Mighty a jowl rub. "Nice little dog you've got here, Frick." He's knuckling our big boy's ears. Seeing Joe and Bubba make nice makes me feel better. Joe's a dog lover. His black-and-white Springer, Sam, is his pride and joy.

I jump right in. "So Joe, what's the verdict here?"

"Frick, you're screwed."

Bob shoots me a crooked smile.

Joe goes on a rant. "Listen. If anyone should be stupid enough to even come inside to look at this godforsaken place, for even a second, for the sake of Lord Jesus, don't let 'em open that closet door in your back bedroom. You'll need to distract 'em. And whatever you do, don't let 'em fill the sink in the kitchen...and keep 'em out of that furnace room in the basement."

I am hanging on every word.

"And don't let 'em flush the toilet downstairs. And, God forbid, keep 'em from filling the tub," he adds.

I should be taking notes.

"By the way, I found a damn mouse behind the refrigerator. Geeesus, Frick! Mow the damn lawn, again, won't you...and plant some red geraniums and pray for a damn miracle."

Is that all, Joe?

Without another word, he hops into his car to drive home to North Lafayette in the neighborhood of Cherry Hill and Telegraph. Finishing the décor around the bar he is building in their basement will occupy the rest of his day. Sipping beers and swapping tales with our favorite bartender at *The Log*, as Joe calls it, becomes my favorite part about visiting Michigan in the years that follow. All of our roommates agree.

Bob and I commiserate briefly. We decide to put a positive spin on his dad's prognosis before we break the news to Kathy.

"Mr. Goodenow was impressed, Kath. He looked everything over. The house checked out just fine," I lie. Thank God she's at work. I tell her that we should have no problem getting our full asking price of $14,500 for the house. "Listen, Kath. If I can finagle a few bucks for the washer and dryer in the basement, I'll take that as compensation for my effort. That work?"

Kathy is delighted.

The next day, I plant a few geraniums before sticking a sign in the lawn and saying a prayer. Later that same afternoon, a young clerk from the neighborhood National Bank of Detroit arrives. He stops me in my tracks.

"I can't believe I'm doing this, but I think I want to buy your house, Mike. My mother believes that your mom is a saint. She thinks it would be good luck for me and my new bride if we bought the house that Marge lived in. We'll pay your asking price, no problem," the young clerk tells me.

Huh?

Equally astonishing is what Kathy decided to do with the miniscule proceeds from the sale. After presenting $500 each to Patrick and to Nino on the day we closed, she marched into the dentist's office two doors down to pay our outstanding balance in full. Apparently the mother of the bank clerk had it wrong. As far as Dr. Clarence Salzberg was concerned, the saint in our family was Kathy, hands-down.

With a bit more help from Bob and a few buddies from the neighborhood, Kathy and Bubba relocate to a perfect two-bedroom apartment in a town called Plymouth. Soon thereafter, Kathy visits a college campus for the first time in her life. At Bob's insistence, I sweet-talk her into coming to Boston. If anyone is deserving of a Harvard-Dartmouth football weekend, it's Kathy, we agreed. On that day, Bob reminded me of the benefit of having a best friend.

Kathy settled in quickly. She is delighted being in the company of all seven of our roommates. They made her feel like part of a family. Come game time, she could not stop giggling. I began to suspect that a friend named Yo might have shared a special brownie with her during halftime. Afterwards, we headed downtown to Durgin Park to enjoy a prime rib feast. Kathy couldn't get over the attitudes of the waitresses, whose Boston sass made our meal all the more memorable.

I had never seen her so happy.

I sometimes wonder if my one and only big sister might have had a mystical connection to Yankee legend Yogi Berra. I could almost picture her wearing a pinstripe jersey with a big number eight on her back on the night she called to ask me what kind of a wedding gift she should buy for some dear friends who had a bridal registry for Royal Doulton China. Considering cost, I told her that a gravy boat might make a nice gift. *"Oh, Michael,"* she replied during that long distance phone call. *"You know I could never afford to buy them a boat!"*

What a doll.

To know her, you would have thought Rosary High offered a major in *"coping."* And although she dated a few cops over the years, she didn't marry one. All in accordance with Marge's final directions; we never took a second mortgage out on the house either.

FORTY

THE MAESTRO

I'm back in Cambridge. It's been two years since I lived in The Yard. After my freshman days in Holworthy, Eliot has become my Harvard home. One of a dozen major residences on campus, it's among a handful of undergraduate houses located on the Charles.

Strolling into our house entry, I'm greeted by a *Harvard hiss*. A time-honored tradition, it's a sound that's normally reserved to express disagreement with professors during large lectures.

This isn't quite that.

"Sssssssss. Hey, Fricksie. Guess who's coming to dinner?"

I didn't even look up. I knew exactly who it was from her accent.

"I have no idea, Pinkie. Let's see...How about Bobby Orr?" I joke.

My friend from Pakistan fancies herself a hockey fanatic. Giggling, she scolds me. "Noo, Fricksie."

I laugh right back. "Of course he's not, Pink. The Bs are at the Garden tonight."

"The *Bob* is not coming, Fricksie. Leonard Bernstein is coming!" she announces with pride.

Huh?

Arms waving, Pinkie is more animated than I had ever seen her. As we stand in our entry, the lilt in her voice makes it echo when she pronounces *"Burn-Stine."*

"Surely you know who he is, Fricksie," she gushes. "He will be in the dining room tonight. *My* sources tell me that he's going to be living here this semester. I've not yet told *Boobie*," she whispers, referring to my roommate Bob. To Pinkie, we were *Fricksie* and *Boobie*, just two peas in a pod. "Joey and Jay and a few others already know," she continues. "You should apply for an independent study. You could do it as a group. Tell me you will do so. Tell me you will! Oh, I wish I could study with him, but my schedule prevents it."

"So, you think *I* should apply?"

"Absolutely I doo, Fricksie."

Now I'm in a quandary. *Oh. Pinkie. Pinkie. Pinkie.*

I can barely strum a guitar.

I'm a Gov major.

He's a cultural icon, a musical genius, an American Original, and he's Marge's Maestro, for God's sake.

Besides, the process is sure to be competitive.

"Of all people, what have you got to lose?"

Hard to argue with that voice from within.

I take to reminding myself how I never once felt uncomfortable, or in over my head, or the least bit out of place at Harvard. Miracle of miracles. Like most everyone around me, I embraced the theory of natural selection and simply let it all evolve. Now Eliot has become my home and each and every one of my roommates has become my family. I'm in a good place, emotionally. Intellectually, physically and spiritually, I love everything about Cambridge. *Lucky boy, Mikee.*

Ok. That's it. I am going for it. To anyone who asks, "Pinkie made me do it."

I'll need to do research, of course. I'm betting I'll also need to write a proposal. Who knows? With that, maybe I'll get a chance to shake his hand, at least. Wouldn't that be something to write home about? God, I wish I could pick up the phone right now and clue Marge in on what's going on. Surely she would have known that her maestro studied at Harvard as an undergrad. She would also have known that he made his orchestral debut with The New York Philharmonic at Carnegie Hall at the tender age of twenty-five. *Whoa.*

Ok. Time to focus. Of course, a proposal is necessary. For that, I take counsel from a friend I would trust with my life. He suggests that I keep it brief. Done.

"   *I wish to study with Leonard Bernstein to explore the sociological transition of Rhythm and Blues to Rock 'n' Roll."*

Twenty words…one simple sentence. It almost feels like I'm cheating.

A short while later, the maestro himself would tell me why he selected the topic he did. "I am intrigued, and I must say delighted, that you didn't spin my wheels by puffing your meager qualifications like other proposals. You got right to the point. I quite like that, actually. Brevity works to your favor, young man. There may be a lesson here, Michael. Good job."

Huh?

Unbelievable.

Did I just get an attaboy for brevity from Marge's Maestro?

I must give credit where credit is due.

The idea of keeping the proposal brief came up during early evening poker. With *Hogan's Heroes* ending on TV 38, the Bruins game is about to begin. Our favorite barkeeps, Frank and Reggie, are heading over to the Casa B to start their shifts as I join the crew in our living room. Phantom and Wrinks. Bob, Lev, and Stevie. Johnny and Tommy. All present and accounted for.

I make casual mention that I'm thrashing over an Independent Study proposal.

Bob lifts an eye to Leverett.

"I think this might call for a wee taste of *Mr. Brooks*, Frick," Lev offers.

A fifth of *Ezra* makes its way from the mantle. Glassware from the Eliot House Dining Room joins bottles of Schaefer on the table.

"Fiery Cross…High-low. Ante up!"

Chips fly.

"Somebody's light."

John obliges.

"Nice try, Stranger."

Clink, clink.

Game on.

Tommy is wearing one red hockey glove. For that he gets *style points*. Very classy. He calls it his "lucky claw," with which he holds his cards. With his right hand, he is holding a *Macanudo*. "I say you go for it, Fricker. Here's how I'd do it." Smoke wafts. He reminds me how he was hell-bent to gain entry into a competitive seminar on the U.S. Presidency freshman year and distinguished himself from the pack by writing a simple one-sentence proposal. *"I am going to be President of the United States one day, so you might as well take me,"* he submitted.

He wasn't joking.

Even as a freshman, Tommy believed one should dream big or go home. So he crafted his proposal accordingly, which earned him a coveted spot in that prestigious first-year seminar.

"Good point, Toe-mas," I thank him. "Cheers."

Done and done.

Brevity works.

It's Monday evening. After a brisk hour of squash at the University Courts near Adams and a *Turkey D* at Elsie's, I'm as ready as I'll ever be for my meeting back at Eliot. I knock on the maestro's door at the stroke of seven. A graduate student greets me. "Mr. Bernstein is on a call."

He points me toward the study.

Sleek and modern, a black desk sits next to a grand piano. A wall of books flanks a red leather sofa. Heavy crimson curtains and dark wood panels cover the walls. A white mantle frames the brick hearth. Two shiny *Harvard Chairs*, looking newly delivered from The Coop, are in front of the fireplace. A stack of dry birch is bundled next to a copper tub filled with kindling, while a Persian Rug covers the floor near the Steinway.

The maestro finds me in the middle of the room. I'm still standing.

"So I guess it's just you and me," he says with a smile. We shake hands.

Mission accomplished.

He tells me he appreciates that I waited for him to arrive before taking my seat since he likes to sit within reach of the piano.

So far, so good, Mikee.

He asks about the origin of my "fabulous surname."

I look at him clueless.

He compensates. *"Fair-ehn-so-vich,"* he offers dramatically. "Your prefix. It's Hungarian. Your suffix is definitely Polish. That much I can tell you. There's Polish in my blood, too, you know. So, tell me about your family. How did you come to study at Harvard?"

Uh-oh.

I keep it brief. *Lesson learned, Maestro.*

I summarize my background as I allow myself to remember it. "You are kind to ask, sir. I'm from Detroit. My parents are dead, so I'm self-directed. I got into Harvard on an orphan ticket."

"Hmm. Interesting. Did you just make that up to impress me?" He smiles as he questions my assertion.

I laugh harder than I should have. "No sir. It's all true, every bit of it, sir."

A moment later, he confides that he was being disingenuous when he expressed interest in my background. Talk about refreshing.

"Don't take this personally, but that was just an attempt to put you at ease. So your brevity is much appreciated, believe me. Well done there. You know, there are people in this world that cannot stop talking about themselves when someone like me poses a question. Just trying to be polite," he counsels.

I'm taken back by his candor. "Thank you, sir."

A moment later, he surprises me again.

"Let's drop the formality, shall we? You will call me Lenny."

"Yes, sir."

Uh…thank you…but I don't think so….

Opting for silence, I become a dutiful scribe.

Rapid-fire, he expounds on matters great and small. My copious note taking is driving his pace. For every question he poses, he is delighted to provide his own answers.

Works for me.

Nannah-Nannah…Nannah-Nannah.
Stop it.

I quiet my mind. The maestro puffs a ciggy.
Game-face, Mikee, game-face. Focus.

He describes a cultural state of arrest that occurred at the moment the atomic bomb was dropped.

Scribble.

He talks about how that led to mass introspection all over the world. "It fed the consciousness of the masses. For my generation, it proved perfectly unfortunate." His eyes lock into mine. Then, waving his arms like he is addressing a concert hall full of patrons, he roars, "My generation *must* have despair!"

I break to stare at my notepad to allow his words to linger.

Breathe, Mikee.

"After Hiroshima and Nagasaki, we became imprinted, emotionally. Can you imagine?" he asks.

"Yes, sir. I mean, no, sir. But I get it," I reply, nervous.

"As a society, we became frozen. Like infants fresh out the womb, we were catapulted into a world of immediacy. People everywhere had to come to terms with a new reality. Life could end tomorrow. In an instant."

Vigorous nod. To that I can relate.

"America fell into an acute state of arrest. As a culture, we demanded immediate gratification. Think about the simplicity of pop lyrics during the 1950s. You know what I mean. It was all about immediacy…boy-girl relationships, that sort of thing."

Scribble. Scribble. I nod.

Digressing, he talks about a Madison Avenue pitch for Bromo Seltzer crystals, which initially prevailed over Alka Seltzer, since those tablets didn't dissolve quite fast enough in the glass for consumers demanding *immediate* relief.

Point taken. Scribble.

He mentions a book called *The Imperial Animal* by Lionel Tiger and Robin Fox. He talks about evolving bio-grammars. "Sociologically and biologically patterns repeat, right, the same way great music repeats."

"Yes, sir."

Silence.

Marge's Maestro is lost in contemplation.

Uh-oh...

"So *here* is a question for *you*, young man."

Long pause.

The silence is killing me. I sit up straight. He lights another cigarette.

"Fire away, sir."

Click. Zippo closed.

"Tell me this," he commands. "Who do *you* think is the pacesetter for the next generation of music?"

Eyebrows raised. Big exhale from the maestro. Smoke wafts to the ceiling.

"Come on. Who is it? You must have an opinion," he pushes. "You are, after all, a Harvard man," he mocks.

I smile. "Of course, sir, I—"

Had it been a year or so later I'd have said David Byrne. Now, before I could spout the words *Lou Reed*, he answers his own question. Again.

Patterns repeat.

"It's David Bowie, right? You were going to say that, weren't you?" he booms.

I smile. *Panic in Detroit* is still stuck in my head from Charles Laquidara's *Big Mattress* on 'BCN this morning.

A discussion about performance art follows. "Ah, David Bowie. Now there's a pacesetter for your generation," he posits as he pauses for another puff. "I'm glad we agree because that's exactly who it is!" He laughs approvingly.

Hair flying every which way; wisps of smoke hover above. He holds his cigarettes in one of a kind fashion, glow-end facing up between his thumb and index finger, like a conductor's baton. To emphasize a point, he shakes the ember theatrically when he's not manipulating his palm upward to take a drag.

"Speaking of generational pacesetters, sir, who would you say are your heroes, from your generation?" I have to ask.

Dead serious, he offers up a wee taste of radical chic, like he is testing me for a reaction. "Other than Malcolm X, you mean?"

I nod.

"That's easy. I can actually answer that one. My Twentieth Century heroes are John, Martin, Robert and Pope John XXIII, in no particular order."

Huh?

It gives me a chill. I shift in my chair. I lock on the sheet music open on the piano: *Bernstein's Mass.*

Suddenly, I'm comforted to remember long ago days filled with clouds of incense and Latin chants, and a mom who loved me unconditionally.

If only she could see me now.

Landing on the subject of artistic passion, the maestro's voice becomes a whisper. His pace slows. He talks about the events surrounding the assassination of President Kennedy ten years before. His eyes are cheerless. Like for everyone who had a heart, that tragedy brought tears from Marge, too.

"I loved him," he offers.

I nod.

"Never had I felt such complete and utter hopelessness," he adds.

He mentions a speech he gave at a crowded Madison Square Garden gala for the United Jewish Appeal on the night Arlington National became home to the Eternal Flame. The words he spoke that were these:

"We musicians, like everyone else, are numb with sorrow at this murder, and with rage at the senselessness of the crime. But this sorrow and rage will not inflame us to seek retribution; rather they will inflame our art. Our music will never again be quite the same. This will be our reply to violence: to make music more intensely, more beautifully, more devotedly than ever before. And with each note we will honor the spirit of John Kennedy, commemorate his courage, and reaffirm his faith in the Triumph of the Mind."

"I was so damn angry. I cannot tell you. I *had* to speak those words that night. I needed to say them out loud…and in public."

Silent, I watch as he pushes his fingers through his hair. Despondent, he shakes his head.

I can offer only a sad smile.

He nods.

I am out the door without a word.

FORTY-ONE

A FORMAL DINNER

Commencement is nearing. Kathy is excited to learn that I had received a nomination for a Fellowship. I am among a handful of finalists for the Michael C. Rockefeller Memorial, which would earn me an interview with a few members of the family, but nothing beyond that, although a wonderful honor, nonetheless.

When Kathy calls back, she tells me that she has booked her flight to Boston. As we're talking, an invitation is slid under our G-11 door. In keeping with a senior year tradition, I have been invited to a dinner at the residence of the House Master. This one will honor a visit by a head of state, Prime Minister Lee Kuan Yew of Singapore. The next afternoon, I stop at the Eliot House Office for a quick hello and to thank our House admin for squeezing my name onto the list.

"Thank Laura," says my friend Edie, who duly records my RSVP.

Proper due diligence follows.

I learn that Prime Minister Lee is the founding father of modern Singapore. I also learn that his country has a human history that spans more than two thousand years, and that his is a notoriously strict jurisdiction, with a government that sanctions corporal punishment. They also enforce the death penalty for narcotics traffickers. And public canings for offenses like vandalism are not uncommon. Minor indiscretions like *jaywalking* and *littering* are dealt with in short order with fines and public ridicule. With its reputation for being the cleanest municipality in the world, I should not have been surprised to learn that there is even a ban on chewing gum in Singapore.

"Don't screw up in conduct, Mikee."

Imagining her voice makes me smile, as my stomach sinks; so heavy-hearted but so very blessed am I.

I also learn that under Prime Minister Lee's stewardship, Singapore has become the most prosperous nation in Southeast Asia. An ardent opponent to the expansion of Communism, he has led Singapore to be a critical ally to Malaysia, Australia, New Zealand, and others, all of which countries are highly supportive of U.S. efforts in Vietnam.

Secret Service check identities at the door as twelve invitees assemble for cocktails in a library near the foyer of the Master's residence. Conversation flows. It's the fourteenth day of May 1975. It's been two weeks since the United States evacuated the American Embassy in Saigon by rooftop helicopters.

The week before, the Prime Minister had been at The White House to express alarm at the speed with which Cambodia was deteriorating. He likened the situation to the *Warsaw Uprising* of 1944, where Poles had to fight without outside assistance. During that siege, more than 150,000 civilians died, most from mass murders. Standing now in our House Master's library at Eliot, the Prime Minister is expressing dismay that hospital beds full of distressed and wounded were being wheeled out of Phnom Penh into the countryside, in an outlandish violation of human rights. He states his concern and fears that in its haste to extricate itself, the United States will turn its back on blatant atrocities. He voices worry that America may become complicit in joining a world community that is taking an *"I told you so attitude,"* in regard to the ruthless actions of Communist regimes like the Khmer Rouge.

Tragically, the Prime Minister's expression of indignation that evening would soon be validated. Mass genocide followed. The atrocities in Cambodia would become known the world over as "*The Killing Fields.*" Two million people perished. Two million.

We are seated now in the dining room, as dinner begins.

An army of white-coat wait-staff enter. They stand at attention. *Interesting.* There are as many waiters as place settings. With no visible cue, they synchronize to serve each guest simultaneously. Every plate touches the tablecloth at the exact same moment. After pausing for a count of "*one-Mississippi,*" the white-coats take a giant step away from the table, all in perfect unison.

They put on quite a show.

I glance at my plate. *Mmm.*

Huh?

What kind of odd-shaped bundle have we here?

I haven't a clue what to do.

I spot a lemon wedge.

It's wrapped in cheesecloth, next to my petite cocktail fork. There's also a ramekin of drawn butter. I hadn't seen one of those since the night of Nino's tenth birthday. None of it makes a bit of sense. *C'mon Mikee. Concentrate.*

The Prime Minister stands to make a toast. "I wish to thank my gracious hosts at Harvard University. As I raise my glass, I am reminded of a proverb I cited for your President a few days ago. It speaks to the attitude of leaders of Communist regimes who feel that those who don't bend must be destroyed. The proverb says, *same bed…different dreams…someone must be wrong.* Please join me in acknowledging the need to work together toward everlasting vigilance against our common enemy."

Eye contact. Hold it. Raise glass slowly.

Clink.

That's better. A sip of Blanc de Noir hits the spot.

I re-focus on my prey.

Perhaps I should befriend it?

Helloooo, mysterious bundle. Aren't you a dandy! Should I cut you in half? Should I fumble with my fork? If a fork, which one do I use?

Maybe I should just dive in with my fingers?

No way. Not at this table, Mikee.

A calming voice makes me smile. Again.

"Just wait until someone you trust takes the lead, and then do as they do."

If only my dining docent from that elegant breakfast years before could see me now.

Focus, Mikee.

That's it. I'll just wait for Mrs. Lee. Who better than she to be my perfect example?

My hands fall to my lap. Back straight, I wait.

Just be patient, Mikee.

I wait some more.

C'mon, Mrs. Lee. Go for it, please.

The theme from Mission Impossible plays in my head.

Boom boom…boom boom boom boom…boom boom….

Stone still, she is unapologetic in waiting for someone else to begin, despite the fact that everyone, including her husband the Prime Minister, is waiting for her.

It's a Mexican standoff!

The stalemate continues....

To my right is my academic advisor, otherwise known as the Eliot House Senior Tutor. She's a terrific woman named Laura, who I suspect was involved in my nomination for that fellowship a few months before. "Just watch *me*," she whispers, too soft for anyone else to hear.

As events evolved, that wasn't the first time in my life that I found myself thanking God for the intuition of a great woman.

Artichokes were a mystery no more.

Two weeks pass in a blur. In preparation for a visit from Mrs. Church, who is joining Kathy to attend my graduation, I decide to take instruction in transcendental meditation. I knew it would make Marge's best friend proud to know that I had adopted one of her rituals, which turns out to be a good thing; one of the best decisions of my young life, in fact.

Bagpipes are marching past each of the upper-class houses. There's a soft rain falling on this misty Cambridge morning on the occasion of my Harvard Commencement. Kathy and Mrs. Church had flown together from Detroit. The day before, I carried my cap and gown in a shopping bag to their hotel lobby. I put it on before rapping on their door. Huge hugs. Wholly unexpected, my loving sister and my mom's best friend present me with a small box containing my Harvard class ring. They even had my name engraved inside the band.

I promise to wear it forever.

FORTY-TWO

HM

Like any other self-respecting Harvard grad, I waste no time finding a place to live after commencement. After sending my diploma back to Detroit with Kathy, I settle in Boston's Back Bay with a wonderful girl, a graduate of Wellesley, who had begun working in advertising the year before. As for me, I take a front-line job in distribution.

I am delivering phone books all over town.

No shame there, whatsoever. Truth is, it's a good workout. Besides, there's no better way to get to know a city, especially its neighborhoods. From *JP* to *Eastie*; *Hyde Pahk* to *Rozzie*; *Mattapan* to *Southie*, I got to know 'em all. Up close and personal. Wicked well.

Like most of our roommates, Tommy also stayed in the Boston area. Married now to his prep school sweetheart, he's taken a position as a community organizer for a group called *Mass Fair Share* while he studies for the LSATs. His beautiful young bride has taken a job at a Little City Hall on a street called Queensberry in the Fens, not far from the MFA. They are renting the upper of a triple-decker near Brigham Circle, which I have no problem locating when I'm invited to their home for dinner. Like every other street in the city, I'd been down it before.

The evening begins with a conversation about taking a marathon 12-hour road trip in their dilapidated Datsun. We decide we'll drive together to Michigan to attend the wedding of one of our Harvard-own in a suburb of Detroit called Birmingham. Perfect. We're also looking forward to visiting Bob's dad Joe at *The Log* in Dearborn Heights with all the boys from Cambridge in tow. Can't wait.

Next on our agenda, a discussion ensues concerning my career plans. Tommy and his no-nonsense bride Biz offer to help me strategize an immediate path. "Gawd, you're delivering phone books, Frick? Really?" She rolls her eyes. Tommy smiles. "Time for a cigar, Fricker." We adjourn to the back porch.

Before my departure that evening, we had all come to the agreement that I should volunteer to work on a campaign for incumbent Mayor Kevin White.

Solid thinking, that.

Since the Mayor's winning margin was less than 8,000 votes, every precinct counted, particularly mine in Ward Five, where elderly turnout proved crucial. All according to plan, a short while after the election, I was hired to work in the new administration. My start date conflicted with an important wedding in Louisiana, which I still regret missing. I hoped my friend would forgive me. Timing could not have been worse from that standpoint.

At least I had gainful employment.

Day one begins on Beacon Hill with an unexpected breakfast meeting at the Mayor's residence, a Mt. Vernon Street townhome, where he lives with his wife Kathryn near Louisburg Square. After a recap of lessons-learned from the campaign, a discussion on future strategies and big picture priorities ensues. The meeting adjourns. By the end of that day I found myself filled with pride that my City Hall career began with a meeting with Hizzoner himself. It sure beats delivering telephone books.

A handful of months later, something else happens that I never could have expected.

End of the workday. I am home at my usual hour. I pop a Bud before settling in to my 7 p.m. routine. Butter knife at the ready, I scoop up the bundle in front of my door to work my way through a stack of junk mail and a few bills, along with something that looks like a wedding announcement.

But it's not.

The Officers of the Bostonian Society

And

Boston 200

Request Your Presence at

The Old State House

For a Special Commemorative Ceremony

To be Attended by

Her Majesty Queen Elizabeth II

And His Royal Highness

The Prince Philip

Duke of Edinburgh

Sunday, July 11, 1976

Half After Eleven O'clock

To be followed by reception

RSVP by June 18th

No. 76

Holy Schmoly.

Subsequent invitations provide more details. The festivities begin on Saturday, with a reception to watch a Procession of Tall Ships on Boston Harbor. The next day will end with a parade on Congress Street. The main event, a Sunday ceremony at The Old State House, will be followed by a private reception and luncheon at City Hall with the Queen and Prince Philip in attendance.

Huh?

I try to imagine how Marge might have reacted had she opened such an invite. It's getting harder by the day to remember her expressions anymore, but I can almost hear her tickled laugh. Then I realize that being invited to attend a reception with the Queen of England is not something to which one can aspire. It's just something that happens. And when it does, all you can do is be on time, smile and look your best.

I can't resist calling Kathy to share this incredible news. Her response is similar to her rejoinder when I told her I had been accepted to attend Harvard.

"Oh, that's nice."

Her deadpan reaction makes me giggle.

Before signing off, she ends our call with a request. *"Just promise me you'll have clean underwear on when you meet the Queen, Mikee. Gotta go. Love you. Bye."*

What a doll.

I laughed so hard I almost wet my pants. Speaking of which, what the hell am I going to wear? *Relax, Mikee. There's plenty of time for wardrobe decisions.*

Excitement gets the better of me.

The following Saturday, I head into town on the Green Line. Park Street Under outbound delivers me to Harvard Square. Strolling down Dunster to Mt. Auburn, I march into *JPress* like I own the place. The salesman gives me a knowing smile. *Fish on.* He looks just like Rod Serling. Go figure.

After fitting me for a dark blue suit for the occasion, I pay way too much for a pale yellow silk tie. No power colors for this boy, not at this little shindig. Afterward I head downtown to Filene's Basement, where I pick out a white, flair-collar, 100% cotton dress shirt, in Marge's honor. I also buy a pair of black wingtips. In deference to Kathy, I chuckle as I pick out a package of pristine silk boxers.

So what if I can't afford any of it?

I can't remember a time when I felt more excited about spending money that I didn't have. I'm betting this is how Marge felt when she went shopping for our extravagant puppy on that Christmas Eve afternoon. It seems like only yesterday. Could it really be ten years ago?

Finishing my junket on street level, I complete my ensemble with a pair of black cashmere socks. As much as I want to look good on this day, I also want to *feel* luxurious in the presence of the Queen.

Huh?

Imagine.

Mikee in cashmere socks! I must be dreaming.

Up and down, from highs to lows, my rollercoaster ride seems never ending. Just the week before, my apartment had been robbed, though pickings were slim. My only treasured possessions were Tony's book on Walter Hagen and one other item. It was something Marge had given me that I cherished as much as anything in the world. For safekeeping, I kept her AA medallion in the top drawer of my dresser, along with my socks and handkerchiefs. Unfortunately, they got it. The size of a dashboard St. Christopher medal, on one side were the letters "*A.A.*" with the words, "*To Thine Own Self Be True.*" Engraved on the flipside was "*Marge F.*" Below that, two letters, "*L.D.,*" were right above Patrick's date of birth. I still smile every time I remember the laugh Marge and I shared on the day she gave me that medallion. At least I have my memories of her, forever.

Standing now at my dining room table, contemplating the events to come, I am feeling as blessed as I ever have in my life. Had that invitation arrived the week before, the thieves might very well have run off with my mail, and I might never have seen my name in calligraphy on that envelope. *Lucky boy, Mikee. Lucky boy.*

Boston Harbor sparkles like a jewel. It's a crystal clear Saturday morning when the Procession of Tall Ships begins. Flags identify countries of origin. Spinnakers billow as multi-masted vessels sail in full glory beneath flumes of spray from fireboats that create a misty gateway. I swear I spot a rainbow. I'm guessing that the Queen and Prince Philip are sitting out on HMY Britannia in the middle of the harbor, enjoying the show. I'm on a pier behind velvet ropes, standing in an exclusive viewing area, enjoying an elegant flute of champagne at ten in the morning. Unbelievable. I'm also savoring my first-ever cucumber finger sandwich, sans crust, no less.

Earlier that week, an advance team from the State Department led a protocol briefing where rules were imparted. "If you find yourself in the receiving line, address Queen Elizabeth II as *Your Majesty. Only* if she is wearing a glove and *only* if she extends her hand to you, may you touch the Queen's hand, *but only in prescribed fashion.* Otherwise, do not under any circumstances touch the Queen. That goes for you, too, Mr. Mayor. Address Prince Philip as *Your Royal Highness.* And to the women, if you are not a British subject, do *not* curtsy."

It was helpful.

Prescribed fashion had to do with a proper touch designed to keep the receiving line moving at a brisk pace. Fingers straight, palm down, raise the hand gently. Touch the Queen's downward-turned palm only with the top of your hand. They were quite clear about that. You did not just grab hers and shake it and start up a little chit-chat. At this reception, protocol would be followed to the letter, the officials from the advance team explained.

After the City Hall reception, I found myself sitting opposite Her Majesty during a parade down Congress Street. I couldn't help but marvel at her ability to sit motionless, gloved hands on her lap, back straight, knees and ankles together for more than an hour. She looked just as she did on the night I fell asleep with the smell of puppy breath all over me. "*...Hold onto that pipedream for me would you, buddy,*" Marge told me the next morning with a giggle while she tickled my armpit for good measure. God love her.

It makes me sad she will never know.

FORTY-THREE

IL PAPA

Short of a championship season, no other occasion could equal the pageantry and excitement generated by Queen Elizabeth's visit, except perhaps for one. The most Catholic city in America is about to greet Pope John Paul II on the heels of his triumphant visit to his homeland. It's been less than a year since his election as the first non-Italian Pontiff in more than 400 years.

His visit will occur one day shy of a bitter anniversary for Boston when a shortstop in pinstripes crushed our collective dreams with what should have been a high-fly single off the monster in left. *Bucky-Effing-Dent.* As rumors of a corked bat continue to circulate, Fenway faithful are still in a funk over that heartbreak a year ago. As far as I'm concerned, the Pope's historic visit is just what we need to put it all behind us.

At long last, I am beginning to figure out that letting go works.

White Banners with yellow script reading "*Il Papa*" festoon lampposts. Throughout the North End, adoring residents toss confetti and flowers from fire escapes and rooftops. Traveling to the South End and then on to Dorchester, the Pope is greeted by the curious and faithful. The crowds are exuberant. Youths hang from light standards; others from signposts. Seniors shout salutations in a dozen languages. The Pope replies in kind. Crowds spill out from homes and storefronts wherever his motorcade travels. The excitement is palpable.

A late afternoon downpour brings out an array of foul weather gear, although not even a near nor'easter could dampen spirits on this day. I can't resist going downtown to check out the scene on the Common, where a crowd of 400,000 have gathered for the Papal Mass. Some have been there all night. Considering the weather, I decide to keep my visit brief. There is no way I am going to get close enough to see Il Papa, anyway. God bless him.

Then something happens.

By Boston standards, it is a small miracle. From the far reaches in the back of the crowd, everyone around me is aware of the exact moment the Pope ascends to the altar as a sea of umbrellas in front of us retracts. There is no prompting or announcement. In a moment of willful spontaneity, in the middle of that torrential downpour comes the most remarkable display of public unselfishness anyone could have imagined. My adopted Boston never felt more alive or more joyous than at that moment. Who wouldn't feel blessed and exhilarated after witnessing such generosity of spirit?

Making my way home, I am beyond the boundaries of imagination no longer. I have been part of a throng in a Pope's faraway presence, surrounded by teeming masses. *You did it, Mikee. You did good.* Telling myself that isn't quite the same as hearing it from Marge, however.

But it will do.

An outbound Cleveland Circle train drops me at my Brighton apartment. I'm living on the inbound side of Commonwealth, just beyond Washington Street.

It feels good to be home out of the rain. A hot shower cures my chill. I flip on the TV. Mass is just ending. Helicopters are still hovering over the Common, recording images of a well-behaved citizenry dispersing back to their homes. God, I love this town.

The published itinerary has the Pope traveling on Commonwealth to the Cardinal's residence at the Archdiocesan Chancery a bit farther outbound. With no chance of catching a glimpse from across the wide thoroughfare, I resolve to stand tall on my curb. I'm content where I am, happy to count the cars in the convoy. I'll cheer from afar, I figure. That will do. I *have* already experienced the miracle of umbrellas firsthand, after all.

Outside my apartment, only a handful of faithful and curious have gathered. I marvel at the size of the crowd creating a crush on the far side of the street, as I spot a stretch of fresh asphalt before me. It's running directly in front of my building in both directions. Just like everyone around me, I am oblivious to what it might mean.

A cortege of motorcycles leads a convoy of black limousines. One of the cars has yellow and white Papal flags flapping above each headlight—and it's traveling outbound on the inbound side of the street. Unbelievable. The Pope's motorcade is about to pass at an arms-length distance from where I am standing.

In the name of the Father, and of the Son, and of the Holy Spirit....

An interior dome light is on.

Unbelievable!

The man who inspires legions of faithful to comfort the poor and dying and feed the sick and hungry looks more like an athlete than the Vicar of Christ, sitting erect in the back seat on the driver's side. When he turns to his left our eyes meet. He smiles and waves, then tosses a tiny "*air blessing.*"

Time stands still.

"Bless me, *Holy* Father, for I have sinned," I pray in Marge's honor. Blissful as I commemorate the biggest Mulligan of both of our lives, I smile and wave right back at him.

Although the Pope's visit lasted less than 24-hours, for days on end, excitement never waned. Moonlighting as a bartender at the old *Plough & Stars* in Cambridge while studying for the GMAT, I had an opportunity to speak with countless patrons, all of whom shared tales of their own experiences during that magnificent Papal visit. From rookies to regulars, my fellow mates Dan, Mary and Barry all heard, as did I, dozens of denizens of the *Plough*, offer up first-hand observations about seeing the Pope, or otherwise being in his faraway presence. For anyone who got close, to a person, they swore he looked directly into their eyes, too.

No wonder I love my adopted city so.

"Start me one more point, wudja Moyke," begs Declan as little Johnnie Began motions for another Guinness as well. Left with two broken arms after falling from atop a light standard, a wee nod of his loaf is all he can manage. From my station behind the bar at the Plough, that works just fine for me.

AAAAAHHH, BOSTON.

FORTY-FOUR

NANTUCKET

Eight Months Later.

It's breezeless and cloudless on the island this morning. Absent marine layer and with tides reversing, the slack-still ocean holds a silky sheen. The roastery in town is bustling. Packed with experts on all things local, consensus among coffee lovers is that the hottest day of the year is upon us.

My last visit to this idyllic outpost came five years earlier, in the company of my college roommates. God love each and every one. As we gathered to celebrate the wedding of one of one of our own, our pal Tommy was about to marry his Milton Academy sweetheart at her family's summer home. A party for the ages ensued when legions of Harvard, Smith and former Milton classmates descended.

Fabulous though brief, our visit lasted just sixteen hours. At daybreak following the reception, we were all summarily rousted and shipped to the mainland, en masse. Slicing through choppy seas on our way back to Hyannis, we had no problem placing blame for our harmless exuberance the evening before squarely on the shoulders of the groom. To a person we agreed that Tommy would happily have accepted our grumblings with his customary cackle had he not been enjoying his first morning of marital bliss.

Now, a handful of years later, I have returned to the scene of past shenanigans to engage in a solo weekend getaway.

No agenda. Just a bit of *R&R* for Mikee.

Except for catching a mid-afternoon ferry to the mainland, the most exciting part of this day will involve digesting every section of The Sunday Globe with my morning coffee. Black, thank you. Heading toward the pier, I spot a sandwich-board sign beckoning near a stand of bicycles. After a brief exchange with the shop's owner, I pick a fender-less one-speed. Sightseeing from atop an old steel-framed Schwinn will occupy the remainder of my visit, I've decided. Nothing like spontaneity when you're on holiday.

Commandeering the bike on foot, I splash through puddles pooling beneath flower boxes along a row of tidy storefronts. Roostertail sprays make red bricks glisten. Overhead, bumblebees buzz baskets of blooms hanging from lampposts. Pretty mommies and proud daddies amble, arm-in-arm, pushing strollers, laughing and cooing. Others pause to admire handiworks of artisans displayed in windows of shops soon to open. Inviting aromas seep through clerestory transoms. The scent of blueberry muffins and dark roast coffees hovers in the treetops. Down the lanes, hydrangea bloom tall and wide. Primrose and honeysuckle spill over mossy sidewalls of stately homes fronted by whitewashed pickets. When a butterfly lands on my handlebars, I realize that this is exactly the way I imagine Heaven would be. It makes me laugh to think that I finally made it.

Once past the cobblestones, I hop aboard. Feeling the soft breeze on my face reminds me just how long it's been since I last rode a bicycle. That would have been back when I buried Duchess. Now *there* is something that I hadn't allowed myself to think about but once since the day it happened. *God bless her*. I pedal.

Road rising before me, my landmark looms ahead. It is sitting atop a knoll, exactly where the bike shop owner said I would find it. Stopping for the view, I straddle the bike in the shadow of that two-hundred-year-old windmill to check my map.

Onward, I push.

Sprawling estate homes dot the countryside. Some have caretakers' quarters, half-again as big as the houses around Faust. Funny, it's been ages since I had given that old neighborhood of mine even a second thought.

Pedal, Mikee, faster.

Heat is shimmering off the blacktop ahead as the Schwinn takes on a life of its own. A voice is rising from the din of rolling rubber. *"Figure out what to hold onto...forever in your heart...for a full life."*

Huh?

I can't believe what I think I just heard. A full life? After my little journey? I challenge anyone to imagine a young life more rich and full of experience than mine, thank you very much.

"So why is your heart so empty and why do you feel so sad?"

Empty doesn't quite describe it.

Truth is, until this very moment, I had refused to admit that I had allowed my heart to be sucked hollow by a destiny for which I never asked.

Why would I risk losing the one connection I treasure as much as life itself by ignoring my mom's deathbed whisper? And why would I forsake all of my memories of childhood by refusing to hold even one in my heart for safekeeping? Isn't that what Marge told me I should build on?

What's up with that, Mikee?

Now, even my memories of her are vanishing. Worse yet, the pit in my stomach won't let me deny that once all my memories of childhood have faded, Marge will forever be gone, as well.

There will be no bringing her back.

Concentrate.
Pedal.
Faster.
Stand.

I'm coasting now.

The warm breeze feels good on my face, as I gaze at the sandy soil blurring with sun-washed grasses. The cloudless canopy above makes me feel like I'm trapped in a fishbowl. *Heads up!* Close call. Sitting to steer, I veer from the asphalt edge, then swerve to glance over my shoulder. At least that old windmill still stands proud. From a distance, it looks less like a granary than a giant pendulum. I can't help but wonder how far its arm would have swung had it begun its descent on that miserable evening, a dozen years before, when I stood alone in that godforsaken funeral home basement.

Oopsie.

With a slam to the brakes I avoid a ditch. Skidding sideways, I careen beyond the bike path edge. I'm flying over the handlebars. *Ouch.* Face plant.

Nice one, Mikee.

Splayed in sand, as I brush a cricket out of my hair, I realize it's my first tumble from a bike since I was seven. That was on a Schwinn without fenders, as well, I remember.

Take a minute. Be still. Catch a breath.

Removing my shirt to wipe my face, all of a sudden I'm back on Faust, in a world that I had long ago stopped caring had ever existed.

It's beyond me why that is.

I am upstairs, outside our bedroom. I'm with Patrick. We are preparing to slide down a well-worn path, step-to-carpeted step, on our resilient little bums. They have become hardened by years of spinning in aluminum bowls while our grammie Claire made chocolate peanut butter fudge from our grandfather's secret recipe. I can smell it. Now dressed and ready to get on with our day, we are preparing to head over to our special neighborhood play spot. We announce our destination as we rumble out the door. *"We're just going over to the rat field, Mom. We'll be back in a couple of hours."*

Marge loves having little boys who know how to entertain themselves.

"Ok guys. Have fun."

This cannot be happening.

It's a picture-postcard morning and I'm surrounded by pastoral countryside, on a beautiful island in the Atlantic, and the only memory I can manage to conjure is of a vacant industrial site across the railroad tracks from a Nabisco Cookie Factory a few blocks from my childhood home? *Seriously, Mikee. Is that all you got for a memory? The rat field? Is that the best you can do?*

Unbelievable.

Wrapping, twisting, I knot my shirt onto the handlebars. Maybe I'll feel better if I let my shoulders bake. Funny, the warmth feels good, but considering my surroundings, it's near impossible to imagine that this could be the same sun that shined down on Patrick and me when we played in the rat field as kids. Those were days when we believed that anything growing out of the ground was worthy of a bouquet for our mom, so we never returned home without bunches of handpicked weeds. Purple fuzzies mostly, and creamy Queen Anne's lace. *At least I can remember the colors.* Upon our return, Marge would drop whatever she was doing at the moment we walked through the door. Responding with big hugs and plenty of praise for us both, she would fill an old jelly jar from the tap and place our offerings on the windowsill, above the kitchen sink, until they drooped. Surely, that's a memory worth keeping. Right? Where the hell has that one been hiding?

I am not sure of anything anymore.

I don't even know if I am heading in the right direction.

Onward, I'm pedaling like I imagine a banshee would while being chased by Satan himself. *Blasted Devil.* I'm losing it. Another voice is rising, but this time it's not coming from some din of rolling rubber or a whisper of wind in my ear. This voice is rising from deep inside me.

"Just let the bad things go."

What bad things?

There *are* no bad things anymore.

I did let them all go, didn't I?

God help me.

Back in town, I head down to the pier. Slack tide no more, lapping waves make pilings glimmer from constant ebb and flow. I can almost hear the universe righting itself, searching for balance, as the sun bounces off the sound. For an eerie moment, I feel like I am in church. Shunning my shades, I rub my eyes as I walk to the edge on the end. I think of my dad for the first time in ages. I tell myself that I loved him. *What's up with that?* Of course, I loved him. He was my father, for God's sake. So why would I feel the need to remind myself of that? Doesn't every boy miss his dad terribly when he's gone? If that's the case, why has it been so long since I have given him even a moment's thought? Is it because he never found time to come to one of my games?

Is that it?

All I can recall now is how he scolded me when he screamed, "*Nothing in life is free.*" That was back when getting a dog to call my own had to remain a distant dream since, he insisted, "he was *allergic.*" Is that why I buried his memory? Is that why I hadn't thought about him in years? Is that what this is all about? Is it because my dad didn't get me a dog?

Talk about emotionally backhanded. Your father is dead, for God's sake, Mikee. Get over it already.

Gripped by a shudder, I stare over the railing. Tiny bubbles are rising from the seabed below, escaping perhaps through creases in mollusks that had buried themselves years before. They are floating, carefree now, toward daylight. Watching them rise is enough to make me remember a genesis of my own, back in the day, when simple chores yielded simple rewards, like a hearty warm breakfast on a weekend morning. I am remembering now. I can see the faithful faces of my teammates' parents who packed-in behind the backstop for opening-day games when I pitched. I remember the melodies of solemn hymns like *Tantum Ergo* and *O Salutaris Hostia*. I remember chanting my Latin prayers in the language of the ancients beneath clouds of bitter-smelling incense. I remember earning a crisp five-dollar bill for *"doing a reading"* as a fourth-grader while serving my first wedding Mass. I remember Saturday night bus rides over to Lyndon and Myers to make new friends with girls from other parishes at an outdoor ice rink called Butzel. I remember how I could barely make my feet shuffle at dance parties when Percy Sledge sang *When a Man Loves a Woman*. I remember holding on for dear life beneath paper lanterns when I danced my first dance to the Beatles' *Yesterday* in some neighbor's backyard. God, it feels good to be back in the company of these memories, so harmless and happy and true. It's beyond me why they have been absent for so long.

The bubbles are floating calmly now atop the placid surface. I wonder how long they will be able to survive there before dissolving into nothing.

Pop!

Pop!

Pop!

Gone forevermore.

A fleeting memory sparks another shiver.

I'm remembering something I had buried years before. Truth be told, I buried it more than once. The first time I did so was the afternoon I sprinted home from football practice, prepared to hear the words, *"Your mom is dead."* I buried it again at my dad's funeral a few days later, sitting in the first row pew of a church packed with people who loved our dad Tony. The last time I buried it was when I learned the sorry truth about what it means for a boy to man a shovel when I dug that grave and said goodbye to my puppy. God rest her soul. Ah, Duchess.

"Let the bad things go, Mikee. Just let 'em go."

Isn't that what Marge had told me? Wasn't that her dying direction? Best I leave it all buried forever, I figure. Right? *Shouldn't I?* It's all so confusing. By burying my childhood I have effectively dismissed my family from my life. It's enough to make me question my sanity. Why would anyone do such a thing?

Breathe, Mikee.

Facing the harbor, I close my eyes to make the sign of the cross. *In the name of the Father...and of the Son...*I say a quick prayer for my dad. It doesn't take long since I know God has heard it before. Now more than thirteen years since his death, I am still praying that the gates of Heaven might open to welcome him.

I hate myself for thinking that.

And that's not all I hate.

I hate these god-awful feelings of guilt that I can't shake, almost as much as I hate the putrid taste of bile rising in the back of my throat that prevents me from saying aloud what I can no longer keep secret. Most of all, I hate that I can't figure out why I am unable to recall what caused me to bury all my memories in the first place.

Blame it on a discordant ring from a buoy out in the harbor; or on the sound of steady lapping from waves kissing pilings. Whatever the reason, the sudden prospect of dealing with the poison inside makes me determined to remember whatever it was that I worked so hard to forget.

Concentrate, Mikee. Concentrate.

Standing now on the end of the pier, I thank my lucky stars that no one can read my mind. *"What kind of emotional lowlife-of-a-boy cries a river over his damn puppy's grave, but sheds not one tear when his own father dies?"*

There. I said it.

What's up with that, Mikee?

God forgive me.

Vomit rising, I lean too far when I spew into the void. I grab the rail to keep from tumbling.

Screw it. Just tumble, Mikee.

Don't listen. Don't listen. I keep my eyes closed. Tight. If I open them, I fear I might lose the will to confront what I buried years ago with my shame.

FORTY-FIVE

DOG WATER FREE

I'm twelve again. It's a year into Marge's illness. I am struggling not to think about that. Climbing stairs has become impossible for her, so she spends every night on the sofa in our living room. "Mikee, I need you to stay up with me, just until your dad gets home and goes to bed. Your father's been a little unpredictable lately. You know that. He's worked up. This whole thing about my condition is eating at him. I just want to make sure that he goes straight to bed. All right, honey?"

"Sure, Mom."

Together we sit.

Calm as we wait.

The clock ticks toward eleven. I can't imagine how hard it must be for my dad, to have to watch the woman of his dreams fade away forever, before his very eyes.

For all our sakes, I wish I could make time stand still.

Ranting and raving, he bursts through the door. It's like I am not even in the room. His gaze is crazy fierce. He rushes her. With no time to think, I jump in. The first of his blows glance, missing their mark. It's then that I realize I can hold my own. Throughout the barrage, I block and push. The look in his eyes hurts more than his roundhouses. He sends me to the floor. "*Get outta my sight!*" he screams.

"*No way, Dad. No way.*" I lunge. My shoulder lands on his belt buckle. Driving hard, I take him down like a tackling dummy. With every ounce of weight I have, I crush against him to pin his arms. His wrists are on the floor. I feel his breath blowing through his teeth as he spits on my face. Reflex. I slam my forearm beneath his chin. The crush to his windpipe quiets him.

Clutching a cushion, Marge stays put.

When I move toward her, I don't know what to expect.

Still down. Eyes closed, my dad is on the floor shaking. Spit is protruding from the corners of his mouth. A minute passes. Then another. And another. Finally, his eyes open. If he'd had a gun, he would have used it, just as I knew that I would have taken a bullet for my dying mom in a heartbeat.

An eternity passes. He mumbles a curse before climbing the stairs to go to bed.

Marge never had to ask me to keep that incident between ourselves. From that moment forward, I wanted to forget about it forever anyway.

I thought I had.

Like much that happened around that time, my dad's unpredictability became just one more thing that Marge and I dealt with together. In the months that followed, I stayed up with her every night, just in case. Night in and night out. A hundred nights in a row. Until this very moment, however, I had no memory of any of it, in particular, our consecutive run of quiet evenings, which Marge and I treated as quality time, just the two of us, sitting on our living room couch, waiting...and waiting. Each night, we would talk until I could no longer keep my eyes from closing. Then, as soon as she spotted headlights in the driveway, she would wake me with a nudge. That was the most excruciating part. We never knew which Tony would be walking through the door.

He came home angry and screaming often, but he never once came at her again, not like that first night. I would later learn that he had been self-medicating with a variety of prescriptions for alcoholism and depression. A few months later, when a heart attack took his life, Marge sat us all down together on the night of his funeral. She looked us each in the eye to be sure that we understood her words. "*Your father was a good man. I loved him and he loved me, just as he loved each of you. Don't ever forget that.*"

I am thinking about young Patrick now, who loved our dad so. As did we all. I am remembering the late morning of Tony's funeral Mass when he slipped over the back of our first row pew to settle beside our dad's mother Mary. At the tender age of eleven, he tried to console his grandmother as she wailed over the loss of her only son, on that day when I could not buy a tear. Weeping together, they held each other close. From my front row pew, I could hear their breaths skip through every tearful minute of that standing room only service inside St. Suzanne Church.

In the throes of another shudder, a welcome resolve rises within. I know now that were it not for that memory, I would never be able to let go of the guilt that's been haunting me. At long last, I can thank God for answering a prayer I never even knew I said. Finally, I can accept the truth. It's ok that I never cried when my dad died, since I now understand that Patrick's tears and the tears of my grandmother Mary were shed on my behalf, too.

Over and out, God. Over and out.

There's a gaggle of boys milling about on the ferry landing. From my position at the end of the pier, they look to be about the age of six. A generation earlier, such a charming assemblage might have been waiting for Mr. Rockwell to paint their portrait. I move close to eavesdrop as a cloudbank forms on the horizon.

They're engaged in a debate. I am guessing they are arguing the merits of where to drop a line in the water until I realize that this is no 'fish from the pier' kind of Sunday. These adorable little ones are having a business meeting. They are haggling over how to sell lemonade. From all appearances, they have no clue. Shy and reserved, they don't even have the benefit of a card table or a sign to advertise their offerings. They can't even manage eye contact. When I step up to order a small paper glass of their finest, they all stare at their shoes.

"That will be a quarter, mister."

Fishing a coin from my baggy shorts, I drop it into the bottom of a clear plastic canister sitting next to their cooler. It looks lonely down there.

"How's it going, guys?"

"Not so good," says the pudgy one, who is the likeness of Heavy when he was six.

"What's the problem, fellas?"

We've been out here all morning, Mister. And you're our first customer," they tell me, sadly.

Being called "mister" makes me smile. I am reminded of Patrick's first days as a young entrepreneur and the havoc he wreaked up and down Faust when he introduced his concept of *surprise haircuts* to unlikely suspects. With that, I take a step back.

There's a large cooler. *Check.*

There's a box of three-ounce Dixie cups. *Check.*

And there's a plastic money jar.

That's it.

For all anyone can tell, this group of precious ragamuffins is just hanging out on the pier. Ferry-goers would have to be clairvoyant to know they had refreshments for sale. Unable to resist, I huddle them around me. We have a little chat. It takes all of a minute to explain my plan to create a compelling call to action. As the boys run off to gather some simple supplies, I head back toward town to return the bike and grab my duffle.

And make a little sign.

The landing is bustling as I ascend to the ferry's top deck. Holding the rail, I gaze out over the pier with no fear of tumbling any more. In front of that band of little ones, there's a long line of customers, all waiting for sips of refreshment. Nearby a horde of doggies, most of unknown origin, mingle happily with purebred-types of Boxer, Bernese and Bulldog, while their owners enjoy a brief respite with new friends out on the pier. Bursting with confidence now, the little boys have become the center of attention. And every time they tip their cooler to fill a small paper cup, they throw a high-five before moving on to the next.

Even over the loud hum from the engines, I can hear them yell in splendid unison, repeating the words from the poster board sign that I delivered when I returned from town.

"Lemonade, a quarter…DOG WATER FREE!"

"Lemonade, a quarter…DOG WATER FREE!"

"Lemonade, a quarter…DOG WATER FREE!"

I squint toward the cloud on the horizon. Sitting atop that puff, someone is greeting me with eyes that sparkle and a smile that says it all. Now, I'm surrounded by happy faces. For the first time in ages, I don't feel alone when I look down upon that gaggle of little boys, with that herd of sweet doggies, tails wagging, all lapping from small bowls like they are enjoying the best thing they had ever tasted. A wisp of breeze. A soft voice summons. I wonder how long it's taken for that whisper to travel from her corner of eternity, so far from this world where nothing lasts forever.

"We're exactly where we're supposed to be."

A salty tear rolls down my cheek to find the corner of my mouth.

Truth revealed. I know now that Marge has been with me all along.

She is with me still.

-The End-

DEDICATION

https://www.theatlantic.com/national/archive/2014/10/the-search-for-the-killer-of-tom-wales-goes-on/381380/

Tom Wales
1952 – 2001

Dog Water Free is dedicated to the memory of my friend of thirty years, Tom Wales, a one-of-a-kind roommate at Harvard College. Were it not for his counsel, I would never have written a properly brief proposal to study with Marge's Maestro, or joined the Mayor of Boston's campaign team, which resulted in my receiving that invitation to attend a reception for the Queen; nor would I have understood the joys and beauty of Nantucket.

Prior to Harvard, Tom was assigned to live with Senator Robert Kennedy's son, Joe, at Milton Academy, in the aftermath of Joe's father's tragic assassination by a handgun during the 1968 Presidential Primaries. From a son of Bobby and Ethel's to a son of Tony and Marge's, Tom Wales made friends for life. That hit home with me on the night he insisted he introduce me to one of Joe's cousins, who was most gracious and kind and generous with her time at the wedding of another of our roommates. "Come on, Frick. Let's go say hello to Caroline."

At first, I resisted. "Please. No need to bother her."

"It's not about you meeting her, Frick. She should meet you. Come on, now."

Typical Tommy.

God love him.

Serving our nation as an Assistant U.S. Attorney in Seattle, Tom Wales enjoyed a distinguished 18-year career with the U.S. Department of Justice. Devoted to his country, to his family, to his job, and to a rich assortment of civic endeavors, he loved his children, Amy and Tom, Jr. completely and unconditionally. In addition to his duties as a Federal Prosecutor, Tom was also a passionate advocate in protecting the lives of at-risk children in the homes of America, where it is twelve times more likely a child will die from accidental handgun violence than in Western Europe, according to Mayor Bloomberg of New York.

As President of *Washington Ceasefire*, a nonprofit dedicated to reducing gun violence through public awareness and common-sense legislation, Tom sought to mandate trigger locks on handguns to protect innocents, young and old alike. On October 11, 2001, Tom was murdered by a handgun. According to the FBI, he was shot multiple times with a Makarov 9mm semi-automatic, equipped with an aftermarket barrel threaded for a silencer, through a window of his home in Seattle's quiet Queen Anne neighborhood while working on his computer in his basement office. Many believe him to be the only Federal Prosecutor in U.S. history to be killed in the line of duty. Seattle's police chief called it an assassination. Soon thereafter, then U.S. Attorney General John Ashcroft established a $1million reward for information leading to the arrest and conviction of his killer. Now, sixteen years later, his murder remains an unsolved mystery. I share the sentiment of my college roommates and all who knew Tom Wales in seeking justice and closure for his family. We do not kill people in our country for doing their jobs, or for having political beliefs, especially if they work in Law Enforcement. This cold-blooded execution cannot be allowed to stand. If you know something, anything, you can remain anonymous. If you have information, for the sake of a beautiful family, get off the couch. Give it up. Rise and save your soul. The FBI and law enforcement need assistance to close the case. Anything would help. Use a disposable cell or a payphone to contact 1-800-CALLFBI, or find a public computer to send an anonymous tip to **WWW.FBI.GOV**.

Toward the end of his life, Tommy visited me in Lake Tahoe often. We would attend my daughters' softball and soccer games and ski Squaw Valley USA together. Whenever I visited Seattle, he would insist we kayak on Lake Union. We always enjoyed fine cigars afterward in celebration of surviving the wake of floatplanes landing nearby during those epic Sunday morning excursions.

The last time I saw Tom was in his Queen Anne kitchen with his dear Marlis by his side. I made dinner, an extravagant red snapper in a shallot-laden raspberry vinaigrette. Tommy baked bread, "The Italian Way," as he called it. Baking bread and perfecting holiday fruitcake recipes were just two of his many passions.

We last spoke on 9/11.

After a brief conversation, he was able to track down one of our college roommates, who had an office in the World Trade Center. "I got him. He's fine," Tommy called back to report. "Thank God, Frick, I just confirmed Amo was out of town. He wasn't in his office today." We chatted briefly. The events unfolding that morning had numbed us both. Given our emotions that day, I was not surprised when he ended our call with the words "Love you, Fricker," when he signed off to attend to our nation's business. My last words to him were "Love you too, Tommy." How lucky am I?

Over the years, he came to know many of these stories. On more than one occasion, he encouraged me to put them in print. "You've had a journey worth sharing, Frick. Even I'm inspired. Let me know when you publish your memoir, will ya?"

So it is in memory of my dear friend that I am proud to have finally done so in print.

Here ya go, Tommy. Enjoy.

Please visit: **www.walesfoundation.org**

EPILOGUE

As Marge predicted, two beautiful daughters were in my future. Claire and Rachel. Both are UC Berkeley grads, and they are the absolute joys of my life. After completing graduate school at Columbia University, Claire is now a Nurse Practitioner near Colorado Springs. Her husband, Justin Ward, is a US Army Captain, MD. My beautiful Rachel recently earned her Master's Degree in Library & Information Science at UCLA. She is married to Sean McBride who is an All-Star, and they all make me so proud.

To their wonderful mom, Maria, good work, kiddo. And to the surrogate grandpop of our two daughters who would never know a grandfather of their own, God bless you Grande Jack Rarig. God rest your soul. Say hello to Marge and Annie for me.

Ed O'Malley, my dearest friend and earliest St. Suzanne Golden Hawks mentor is a pediatric ophthalmologist in Grosse Pointe, Michigan, where he lives with his wonderful wife Judy. Their children, Erin and Kevin, have been outstanding role models to my girls over the years. Ed changed my life forever when he insisted that I apply to Harvard at a time when I had no clue what might lie ahead. In addition to his duties as a Chief of Staff within the Henry Ford Health System, Ed has donated years traveling the world with PROJECT ORBIS, a nonprofit humanitarian organization devoted to blindness prevention and treatment and the exchange of medical knowledge worldwide in developing countries.

To my anonymous benefactors, Dr. Cy Collins and family, who made it possible for me to attend Detroit Catholic Central High School, thank you. It feels good to say that formally. And to all my CC family, as well my friends from St. Suzanne and beyond, I hope this finds you well. Let me hear from you via **www.dogwaterfree.com**.

Mrs. Church died in 1989 at the age of 76. Three years before, she began studying Mandarin so she could converse with her Chinese doctor in his native language. A member of the Founder's Society of the Detroit Institute of Arts, in her last year she was attending community college to study geology. Thanks to her numerous visits to California when our girls were babies and beyond, she became *Nudgie* to Claire and Rachel.

Joe Goodenow's son, Bob, is godfather to Claire. A former Harvard Hockey captain, he also served as the Executive Director of the National Hockey League Players' Association for a memorable 15-year stint. Firm and tough like his dad, a more reliable, loyal friend one could not be, as he has proved time and again. He and his wife Wendy are the real deal. I can still remember the look on his face when his dad said, "Frick, you're screwed," after inspecting my childhood home. I still light candles for Bob's dad Joe and for his mom Rosie whenever I visit St. Patrick's Cathedral, just as I do for our friend Pinkie, who insisted on calling us "Fricksie and Boobie" a decade before the world would come to know her as Pakistan's Prime Minister, Benazir Bhutto. To her family, her friends from Harvard still mourn her loss.

My lifelong friend and co-conspirator in the cement mixer caper, Lee Wilson is the son of Bunny and Wil and brother of Anne and Beth. He is godfather to Rachel.

In stark contrast to a handful of Christmas mornings alone after Marge died, my memories of exceptional holidays in Corning, New York remain vivid thanks to my dear friend and college roommate, Amo, and his wonderful family. I experienced some of the most memorable holidays of my life in the southern tier of New York because of the kindness of Big Amo, Ruthie, Mory, Robbie, Sarah, Quincy, a Basset named Linus, and two Newfies, Flower and William. I will never forget those holidays, as well as summertime in Marion, and how effortlessly all of the Houghton's made me feel like a part of their family. Thank you Big A and Dear R.

Thanks to another roommate Bill, son of Big Mo Gray, who I am sure remembers Sunday brunches in Dedham, hosting Bo and Frick, where we were introduced to the pleasures of Beef Wellington, thanks to Bill's terrific mom.

I will also never forget my Massachusetts summers, poolside at Stevie's in Concord, thanks to the kindness of Big Prill and Big George Kidder.

To my dearest friends, also roommates, Leverett S. Byrd, son of Emily; and William Snow Harwood, son of Nancy, who introduced me to the joys of Chestnut Hill and to the islands off the coast of Maine, where Tommy also summered, and where I was honored to have been included for end-of-season gatherings and summer fests on North Haven and Vinal Haven. In contrast to my childhood "turkey days" in Detroit, I'll also never forget a most joyous Thanksgiving celebration at Lev's grandfather's farm in Dover, Massachusetts, where I experienced a tradition like no other, which I now share with my own daughters whenever we are together on that Thursday holiday. Seated at the head of the table for afternoon dinner, Lev's grandfather, a beloved former U.S. Senator and three term Governor of Massachusetts, sang *"Bicycle Built For Two"* to his bride Alice and for the entire grouping of children, grandchildren and friends that filled the dining room at his magnificent *gentleman's farm.* At song's end, we broke into wild applause just before dinner was served. It's a great memory that I carry with me still. In fact, I now start to loosen my own vocal chords whenever there is a turkey in the oven, thanks to that fondly remembered Thanksgiving at the home of Senator Leverett Saltonstall. Thank you, Lev and Cath and Dickie and Ames and Harry and your families. God love you all.

To John Stranger of Dorset, England son of Daphne Mae and Neville and one of my earliest editors, I love you, man. Go Sox.

To all my boys from Harvard—Stevie, Billy, Lev, Bill, Bo, Johnny, Mo, Felix, Amo; to my Holworthy roomie Johnny G; and to our extended clan from Eliot, especially Mac, Yo, Kenny, Smitty, Denny, Las, as well as Dr. Jimmy and his entire Winthrop House posse, to name a few, I love you all and I will see you soon in my travels. And to lovely Julie Rooney, whose friendship I cherish, I pray a visit to see you in Hawaii is in the offing soon.

To Biz, Ricky, Kitty, Amy and Tom, Jr., I think of you often. You are in my prayers.

To Ted and Lisa Simons and their boys, I could not have done this without you.

To all my friends, old and new, accept this as a call to action. Let me know you are well. Visit me at **www.dogwaterfree.com** .

Kathy is fine, although she lost her cherished husband to pancreatic cancer a few years ago. He was buried with full military honors, which made Kathy, and me, very proud.

Patrick lived a full life. He passed away in 2014, with our friend, Father Joseph A. Gagnon, by his side in his final days.

Nino left the seminary before his ordination to join the Peace Corps. After working on Africa's Ivory Coast, he moved to Southeast Asia where he has resided for decades.

Acknowledgements

To my Mexico City amigos, Alfredo and Gina and to the entire Miguel family; To Phillip Mitteldorf of Santa Barbara; To Ed McGowan of Atlanta, whose friendship has been steadfast since CC days; To Judy Bergeski of Livonia; To Scott Turlington of Boise; To the entire family of Rooney's in Portola Valley and beyond; To my friend Taylor, congratulations, buddy. See you in Cambridge. To Gun Ruder and to everyone at the Agassi Foundation for Education, a most worthy endeavor that I encourage all to support; and to my editor, Kathleen Marusak of Los Angeles, AKA Kat, whose help and direction has been invaluable. Thank you all.

Discussion Questions

1. Everyone in the story faces challenges. What was the single biggest challenge facing each member of Mikee's family?

2. What role does alcohol play in the story? In what ways is it portrayed as both a positive and negative factor?

3. What role does fate and destiny play in the story?

4. It has been said that it is necessary "to own and honor the child who we *were* in order to love the person we *are*." It's also been said that the only way to do that "is to own your experiences and emotions from childhood and honor that child's feelings." How does that fit with your own experience?

5. Emotional wounds run deep. Are you surprised that Mikee repressed so many memories of his childhood for so long?

6. It's fair to say that Mikee's dad Tony had his demons. What were his strengths and weaknesses, his flaws and contradictions? Is rage ever justifiable?

7. What were Marge's greatest qualities? Could you relate to her character?

8. Years before Marge knew she was dying she placed her faith in Mikee when she introduced the concept of *disappearing*. Based on what you now know about Marge, is it any surprise she did so?

9. Is DOG WATER FREE a happy story or a sad story?

10. How important was it for Mikee to find closure by coming to terms with his guilt for having never cried over the death of his father?

- To join the discussion and meet up with Mikee visit: WWW.FACEBOOK.COM/DOGWATERFREE

See you there.

About The Author

Michael Jay was born at Detroit Henry Ford Hospital. He attended Detroit Catholic Central at 6565 West Outer Drive, with help from an anonymous benefactor. He is a graduate of Harvard College. He earned his MBA at Northeastern University in 1983. His coming-of-age memoir has earned praise as "a mother-son memoir of lasting consequence" by a past President of the Women's National Book Association. His book is dedicated to his college roommate, Tom Wales, who plays a pivotal role in his story, and who many believe to be the only Federal Prosecutor in U.S. history to have been killed in the line of duty. Michael lives in Idaho.

Made in the USA
Lexington, KY
08 January 2018